David,

Keep the F

PEACE,

[signature]

P.S. Bless you for all
your help on this'.

LEADERS ARE URGING ALL AMERICANS TO READ
AWAKEN THE AMERICAN DREAM
by Charles V. Douglas, J.D., CFP®

"As Chief Spiritual Officer of The Ken Blanchard Companies, I strive to positively impact the day-to-day management of people and companies as they pursue the American Dream. Charlie Douglas does an outstanding job of demonstrating that we need both spiritual and financial capital to realize the Dream. A must read in today's trying business climate!"   **—Ken Blanchard, Ph.D.,**
Bestselling Coauthor of *The One Minute Manager*®

"It has often been said that no one on their deathbed wished they had spent more time at the office. Relationships are what truly matter—both human and divine. This book's chronological historical analysis through this lens is fascinating and insightful, and consistently shows that happiness is truly never found in the wallet, but rather lies within the heart."   **—Dr. Stephen Covey,**
Author, *The 7 Habits of Highly Effective People*

"God created us to be successful, but true success cannot be measured by dollars alone. Charlie Douglas puts readers in touch with what it means to be successful, and how to pass on a meaningful legacy. In the past few years, many people have been troubled by the lack of business ethics, but there is no such thing as 'business ethics'—there are only personal ethics and they are the underpinnings of the American Dream."   **—S. Truett Cathy, Founder of Chick-fil-A**

"As a free nation, Americans have the opportunity to reach for their dreams based on the right to life, liberty, and the pursuit of happiness. This timely book serves as a powerful reminder that the foundation of the 'American Dream' depends upon values, virtues, and the Creator who endowed us with our unalienable rights."
—Zell Miller, United States Senator

"Charlie Douglas has tackled, head on, two of the most important issues facing America: how have we so massively lost our way and what role spirituality and religion can play in fashioning values that will right us."
—Charles B. Knapp, Former President of the University of Georgia

"*Awaken the American Dream* is right on the money!"
—**Dyan Cannon, Actress**

"Charlie Douglas does a great service in *Awaken The American Dream.* In this timely book, he dispels the myth that business is inherently corrupt. He proves that by keeping all things in perspective—from your spiritual life to your relationship with your family—you can make money, live a full life, and leave a lasting legacy. Investors should read this book, if for no other purpose than to keep themselves grounded in those fundamental principles upon which our nation was founded."
—**Jack Kemp, Empower America**

"Charlie Douglas warns us that 'we are losing touch with the need to develop lasting wealth based on enduring values.' Right on! He reminds us that the American Dream has never merely been about the acquisition of wealth—but about living lives of virtue, faith, and service to our fellow man. A timely message in an age of corporate scandals." —**Ed Feulner, Ph.D., President of the Heritage Foundation**

"Charlie Douglas's new book is a must read for all who want to be successful by leading a value-centered life. It is a virtual manual on how to do well and do good by living a life of integrity."
—**John R. Seffrin, Ph.D., CEO, American Cancer Society**

"A powerful and much-needed examination of the true American Dream, Charlie Douglas's book couldn't be more timely. America *needs* this book; we need to rediscover and celebrate the majesty of the American capitalist system, and fully appreciate the financial and spiritual freedoms we enjoy. *Awaken The American Dream* covers this topic in more depth and with more clarity than any book I've seen. An absolute, one-of-a-kind must read for every American, regardless of political persuasion."
—**Doug Wead, Former Special Assistant to President George H. W. Bush, Author of *The New York Times* Bestseller *All the Presidents' Children***

"Impossible, but here it is all in one volume: inspiration, education, history, theology, and mini-biographies of the giants that shaped our great country. Tremendous!"
—**Charlie "Tremendous" Jones, Author of *Life Is Tremendous***

"*Awaken The American Dream* is a must read for anyone looking for a roadmap to achieving their dream and creating an unstoppable legacy."
—**Cynthia Kersey, Bestselling Author of *Unstoppable***

"The American Dream is accessible to anyone who understands the basic values and principles upon which the American republic was founded. In this book, Charlie Douglas provides deep, enriching insights and ideas that make you want to pursue the vastness of the Dream with renewed vigor. It is an inspiring and uplifting tribute to all that is good and great in America."
—**Brian Tracy, Bestselling Author of** *Maximum Achievement*

"Charlie Douglas is an extraordinary person, and his book reflects that. After reading it, I came away feeling like I could go and start my life all over again, and do it better, with more love for my fellow man—even at this late age. It's a book you'll want to read, reread, and pass on to your children and grandchildren."
—**Shirley Jones, Academy Award Winning Actress**

"In the rush to capitalize on ever-expanding financial markets, many people neglected the truly important things. Charlie Douglas exposes the cost of that thinking, and reveals the joy that flows from filling the voids in your spiritual and personal life. He makes it plain… that morality and markets can and should be intertwined."
—**William J. Bennett, Bestselling Author of** *The Book of Virtues*

"There is a widespread belief that making money is somehow at odds with making a connection to the higher aspects of life. In this book, Charlie Douglas leaves readers literally more awake, more able to see clearly that succeeding in business is not the goal but, rather, a part of the journey."
—**Gavin de Becker, Bestselling Author of** *The Gift of Fear* **and** *Fear Less*

"Capturing the spiritual to be successful in today's world is essential. Charlie Douglas in *Awaken the American Dream* captures it in a way that is applicable to everyone who desires to have an impact and succeed."
—**Herschel Walker,**
Former NFL Running Back and Heisman Trophy Winner 1982

"*Awaken The American Dream* would make a good gift to Christian business students or those graduating and ready to enter the fray."
—*CBA Marketplace*
Official Magazine of the Christian Booksellers Association

"*Awaken The American Dream* addresses a very timely subject."
—**Steve Forbes,**
President and CEO of Forbes Inc. and Editor-in-Chief of *Forbes* **Magazine**

"Charlie paints a wonderful kaleidoscope of the true American Dream. He shatters the 'Madison Avenue Myth' and enthusiastically articulates the Real American Dream: Being excellent stewards of God's resources to accomplish His purposes. A must read for 'Serious Dreamers.'" —**Steve Franklin, Ph.D., Author, TV Commentator, and Sr. Vice President of New Business Development, Wells Real Estate Funds**

"In *Awaken The American Dream*, author Charlie Douglas has re-established, and with considerable style, the proper continuity between God, personal integrity, and true wealth. By weaving together an entertaining history of our country's economy and its best-known business moguls, with an equally fascinating chronicle of American morals and values, Douglas achieves a portrait of contemporary America that not only clearly defines our dilemmas, but also reveals practical solutions already built into our way of life. And most importantly, he shows how belief in God and God's influence over individuals, when welcomed, can lead us to a future prosperity— not only a prosperity of goods, but a prosperity of spirit. This book will engage your interest and enlighten you, from beginning to end." —**John F. Donoghue, Archbishop of Atlanta, GA**

"Charlie Douglas has written a compelling account of the spiritual corruption of the American Dream. He provides us with a road map for restoring virtue and goodness to personal business enterprise in the context of a fascinating history of America's institutions. A must read, full of Charlie's sincerity and passion." —**Steven T. Levy, M.D., Holland Professor of Psychiatry, Emory University**

"The work of Charlie Douglas in *Awaken The American Dream* should be mandatory reading for every American. Balanced, honest, and carefully researched, Charlie has written a book which may literally change our nation's perception of 'the American Dream' in a most profound and positive way." —**Linda Forsythe, Publisher, *Mentors Magazine***

AWAKEN
THE
AMERICAN
DREAM

★ ★ ★

Embracing Values That Lead
To Lasting Wealth

★ ★ ★

Charles V. Douglas, J.D., CFP®

A Possibility Press Book

AWAKEN THE AMERICAN DREAM

Charles V. Douglas, J.D., CFP®

Published by
Possibility Press
possibilitypress@aol.com
www.possibilitypress.com

Available to the Book Trade from Ingram/Spring Arbor
and Baker & Taylor

1   2   3   4   5   6   7   8   9   10

Publisher's Cataloging-in-Publication
(Provided by Quality Books, Inc.)

Douglas, Charles V.
    Awaken the American Dream: embracing values that lead to lasting wealth/Charles V. Douglas.
    p. cm.
    LCCN 2003107025
    ISBN 0-938716-33-6 (cloth)

    1. Capitalism—Religious aspects. 2. Capitalism—Moral and ethical aspects—United States. 3. Wealth—Religious aspects. 4. United States—Economic conditions. I. Title.

HB501.D675 2003   330.12'2
                                    QBI03-200436

Manufactured in the United States of America

Dedication

This book is dedicated to all of those virtuous individuals who have gone before us, whose selfless spirits left a rich legacy for generations to come. With a firm reliance on the protection of Divine Providence, they mutually pledged to each other their lives, their fortunes, and their sacred honor. And especially to our friend, Deb Connelly, who courageously battled leukemia for many years.

Table of Contents

You CAN Live the American Dream!
By Dr. Robert H. Schuller

Charlie Douglas has written a most timely book. Anyone who wants to live the American Dream and make this a better world needs to read it.

He describes the foundation of the Dream, and how our Founding Fathers relied heavily on God. Charlie traces the erosion of that reliance as the Dream was passed down through the three adult generations.

This book will increase your understanding of why we are at a critical time, and what we need to do about it. The message will resonate with everyone who cares about this country and wants to see it get closer to God.

Arvella and I started out in 1955 with only $500, when I began preaching from the roof of a drive-in theater. With a BIG dream, prayers, and the help of many people, we overcame seemingly insurmountable odds. We did it and so can you!

Read this book, take its message to heart, and live the dream God has for you. If you can dream it, you can do it.

God loves you and so do I!

Robert H. Schuller

Dr. Robert H. Schuller
Founding Pastor, Crystal Cathedral Ministries
www.hourofpower.org

"The liberty we prize is not America's gift to the world; it is God's gift to humanity. We have faith in ourselves—but not in ourselves alone. We do not claim to know the ways of Providence, yet we can trust in them, placing our confidence in the loving God behind all of life, and all of history."

—President George W. Bush
2003 State of the Union Address

Chapter 1

What Is the American Dream?

"When our country was founded,
the pursuit of both spiritual and financial capital
largely represented the essence of the American Dream."
—Charlie Douglas—

There are those who may say that the American Dream is becoming a thing of the past. But I believe we have just lost touch with what it is and how to achieve it. The vastness of the fundamental Dream is slumbering—a giant ready to be awakened.

Material wealth is the hallmark of capitalism, and it has become the primary focus of the American Dream. But America began as a country that offered the promise of both religious freedom and economic opportunity. When our country was founded, the pursuit of both spiritual and financial capital largely represented the essence of the American Dream. It allowed those visionary pioneers the liberty to worship their Creator through inspired enterprise, yielding prosperity grounded in faith and virtue.

Over the course of time, the American Dream came to represent a social ideal which stressed the importance of equality and material prosperity. The phrase itself became popularized in Horatio Alger's *Ragged Dick*, published in 1867. A rags-to-riches story about a poor orphan who made it big, Alger's classic puts forth the notion that the American Dream was available to anyone willing to work hard and embrace noble values.

For most of America's history, the American Dream was seen as a by-product of a well-ordered and virtuous life, not just a pot of gold at the end of the rainbow. The emphasis was on building spiritual capital with the belief that, through creative enterprise, our Creator would provide enough financial capital along the way. Since America's promising beginnings, the Dream has meant different things to various generations. But for many, the original concept of the American Dream seems to be dormant today.

Material wealth is not contrary to the America Dream; it is an essential component. Yet, when the pursuit of material wealth alone becomes the Dream, we do an injustice to the Dream and limit its possibilities.

The #1 International Bestseller, *Who Moved My Cheese?* by Spencer Johnson, M.D., describes a world where mice and mouse-sized humans react differently to change when the cheese they love is moved to another part of the maze. As Ken Blanchard, Ph.D., describes in the foreword, Cheese is "a metaphor for what we want to have in life, whether it is a job, a relationship, money, a big house, freedom, health, recognition, spiritual peace, or even an activity like jogging or golf." Cheese to me represents pursuing what you believe will truly bring happiness to yourself and others. In a sense, Cheese represents the richness of the American Dream.

During the 1990s, millions of us aimed at a limited American Dream by trying to amass financial capital in a raging bull market, while growing spiritual capital often took a backseat. But amassing financial wealth alone didn't bring the happiness many thought it would. In many cases, it failed to enrich our lives and bring about the security we desired.

Since the beginning of the new millennium, our self-assurance has been badly shaken as our world has changed. A brutal bear market, September 11th and the ensuing War Against Terrorism, "Enron-like" scandals, and even indignities within the Catholic Church have pounded away at our already vulnerable institutional base. In our unstable world, we sought reassurance from unsteady institutions which, in some cases, only left us feeling more uneasy. As 2002 came to a close, Gerald Celente of Trends Research Institute in Rhinebeck, N.Y. said, "We have never seen anything like this before. So many people have lost so much trust in so many institutions at the same time."

The dwindling spiritual capital and moral fiber being fashioned by our ailing institutions has caused some to question if we are still "One nation under God." Feelings of fear and envy, rather than love and charity, often reside within us in an increasingly materialistically focused world. America is fast becoming a culture where accumulating economic assets is viewed as more important than cultivating meaningful values and virtues.

Our current concept of wealth is primarily material based. In fact, material wealth is now the DNA of capitalism and the focus of the American Dream. This limited view, however, is proving to be problematic.

Consider the disturbing observation made in the February 2003 issue of *Fast Company* magazine: "Between 1970 and 1999, the average American family received a 16% raise (adjusted for inflation), while the percentage of people who described themselves as 'very happy' fell from 36% to 29%.... We are better paid, better fed, and better educated than ever. Yet the divorce rate has doubled, the teenage suicide rate has tripled, and depression has soared in the past 30 years. The conclusion is inescapable: Our lifestyles are packed with more stuff, but we lead emptier lives. We are consuming more but enjoying it less."

Madonna, the "Material Girl," now middle-aged, recently reflected on the short-sightedness of her view of the American Dream: "Take it from me. I went down the road of 'be all you can be, realize your dreams,' and I'm telling you that fame and fortune are not what they're cracked up to be. We live in a society that seems to value only physical things, only ephemeral things. People will do anything to get on these reality shows and talent contests on TV. We're obsessed."

This book is for today's adult generations, namely, Retirees, Baby Boomers, and Generation Xers. But it is not designed to help you achieve financial wealth alone. It is about coming to terms with the heritage entrusted to us and revitalizing the greatness of the fundamental American Dream. In this manner, we can regain our purposefulness, make a bigger difference in the world, and leave a legacy of truly lasting wealth.

Lasting wealth depends on meaningful values and virtuous conduct. Both should support and reflect a strong connection to our Creator—the source of all love. To realize lasting wealth, we need to reconnect with the greatness of the spirit on which America was founded.

For nearly 20 years, I have been counseling people on matters of monetary wealth as both a lawyer and a financial advisor. I offered what I thought was "comprehensive planning" by recommending prudent financial and legal vehicles to help clients achieve their material goals. Shortly before I wrote this book, however, I began to realize that my services were actually too limited. They often ignored the core values of those I sought to help. Yet these essential values are precisely what are needed to drive the whole planning process.

Born near the end of the Baby Boom, I arbitrarily chased after bits and pieces of the American Dream for most of my life, unaware of the Dream's true essence. It seemed as though Jesus, in Matthew 6:24 and Luke 16:13, had spoken His words of admonition directly to me: "No one can serve two masters. He will either hate one and love the other, or be devoted to one and despise the other. You cannot serve God and mammon [wealth or property]."

I can assure you that I had noble intentions, even though they did little to dispel Jesus' warning. But when I set my sights squarely on achieving financial prosperity, I often felt uneasy. My pursuit and realization of material gain did little to satisfy the restlessness stirring in my soul. The more financial success I had, the more I seemed to become aware of the rumpled person outside my car window—the one with the dog-eared cardboard sign that read: "Homeless. Will work for food."

On the other hand, when I pursued my spirituality foremost, my ego frequently sounded the alarm that reminded me that I was letting the material world pass me by. I could relate to the plate-spinner on *The Ed Sullivan Show*—caught between two poles precariously placed at opposite ends of the stage, frantically running back and forth to keep both of them spinning.

It looked to me as though the American Dream was being pursued by a lot of people who were primarily concerned with logging the right entries into their resumes, looking for appropriate centers of influence to advance their careers, and trying to secure enough assets for early retirement. But I couldn't point an accusing moralistic finger at others when I knew deep down that, in some ways, I, too, was doing much the same.

I am happy to tell you that I have come a long way in my journey, but there is still much to be done before it ends. With God's grace, I am encouraged that I can make a difference to you in your journey toward a richer, more meaningful life.

Agreeing with the ideas in the following pages is not as important as fashioning your own opinion. As you read this book, reflect on the importance of financial and spiritual capital and the heritage with which your generation has been entrusted. Think of ways to invest your life's energy to reinvigorate the American Dream and build a legacy of lasting wealth.

Perhaps most importantly, ponder how and where our Creator fits into your quest for the American Dream. Although many of our public institutions would indicate otherwise, Americans are still a religious people. According to recent Gallup Polls, more than 90 percent of Americans reported they believe in God. More revealing is the fact that 77 percent of Americans believe the overall health of the nation depends a great deal on the spiritual health of its people. George Gallup, director of the Gallup International Institute, recently said, "You cannot really understand America if you do not understand her spiritual underpinnings."

In President George W. Bush's 2003 State of the Union Address, he closed with these words: "Americans are a free people, who know that freedom is the right of every person and the future of every nation. The liberty we prize is not America's gift to the world; it is God's gift to humanity. We have faith in ourselves—but not in ourselves alone. We do not claim to know the ways of Providence, yet we can trust in them, placing our confidence in the loving God behind all of life, and all of history. May He guide us now, and may God continue to bless the United States of America."

The American Dream isn't a thing of the past—its future rests in our hands. Let's awaken it!

"It is not wrong to want to live better; what is wrong is a style of life presumed to be better when our actions are directed towards 'having' rather than 'being,' and which wants to have more, not in order to be more but in order to spend life in enjoyment as an end in itself."

—Pope John Paul II

Chapter 2

The Millionaire Fixation

"We made books like The Millionaire Next Door *and* Rich Dad,
Poor Dad *runaway bestsellers. We tried to catch a glimpse of who
the wealthy were and how they made it."*
—Charlie Douglas—

As the 1990s drew to a close, I recall beginning each day with a 6 a.m. workout at a nearby gym. The bull market was charging ahead, fueled by venture capital and the perceived bright future of the Internet's new-economy stocks. In those days, morning workouts were actually kind of fun.

Most days, I would begin my routine with a half hour of cardiovascular exercise on the treadmill, while watching CNBC's *Squawk Box* on the television set overhead. Everywhere I looked, people were working out and watching some type of financial program. There was electricity in the air surrounding the capitalization of the Internet and how much IPOs (Initial Public Offerings), like eToys, would appreciate on the first day of trading.

I would listen attentively as CNBC's Maria Bartiromo described market conditions before the opening bell. She often said, "Once again folks, it's all about technology as the sector is set to open higher." During those golden days, I would say to myself, "What an opportunity to be living and investing during the build-out of the Internet's infrastructure."

Even so, I never really believed in the dotcoms. I reasoned there was a gold-rush mentality surrounding the new economy stocks and figured that most who "panned for gold" were sure to come up empty-handed. But the infrastructure, or backbone, to the Internet—now that was a different story. After all, during the

1849 California Gold Rush, those who supplied pickaxes and shovels were the ones who made the money.

With blue-chip companies like Dell, Cisco, Lucent Technologies, Oracle, Intel, Microsoft, AT&T, Sun Microsystems, Nokia, WorldCom, and a host of others, how could anyone miss over the long-term? These were real companies with solid earnings, viable business plans, and capable leaders. Besides, Wall Street pundits and analysts were falling all over themselves. They eagerly told us that it was just the first inning, as they overwhelmingly assigned many tech and telecom companies with strong buy ratings.

A seven year old calls CNBC and wants to know from today's guest analyst his outlook for Lucent Technologies, which is trading in the mid-sixties. Everyone on the program smiles and remarks how wonderful it is that a child is getting such an early start at building her financial acumen. Of course, they confidently tell her it is definitely a buy over the long-term.

I stop the treadmill and ask myself if anyone has the common sense to say to her—"Hey, kid, what are you doing calling us? Shouldn't you be in school, out playing, or watching cartoons? You're only seven."

As I stand motionless, I recall that when I was seven, my limited financial insight consisted of prematurely yanking out a baby tooth so the benevolent tooth fairy would grace me with 25 cents. I thought that was particularly shrewd thinking, as it was all the money I needed to catch up with my superheroes, *Spiderman* and *Superman,* in the latest *DC Comics* books.

I wipe the sweat from my face as I look around the gym. People are slurping their bottled water as the treadmills quickly turn underneath their feet. I whisper to myself, "My God! We look just like Pavlovian rats running on our wheels, waiting for the next stimulus of pleasure from green up-arrows, as we mindlessly stare at the moving ticker tape on the TV screen."

Many of us were more physically fit on the outside than we were on the inside. Perhaps we were spending a lot more time at the gym than at our places of worship? I began to wonder, "Is this life for the body or the soul?"

I asked myself two daunting questions: "Am I a body that has a soul? Or am I an eternal soul that has temporary use of this body?" As I think about the answer, I start feeling uncomfortable. I try to avoid the issue by quickly moving over to the bicep machine and crank out ten reps.

Let's Create Something v. *"Show Me the Money"*

As I watch my biceps in the mirror, which have gone nowhere in 20 years, I think about an article I had recently read in *Forbes* magazine about Silicon Valley. The writer told of a luncheon he had in Palo Alto with a forty-something CEO who said flat-out, "Ten million dollars is chump change...I don't know anyone who thinks one million, five million, or ten million is enough!" The article ends with some thoughts from a venture capitalist who says, "The newer people are motivated by wealth. It's troublesome. It's 'What's in it for me?' instead of 'Let's create something.'"

I ask myself, "If we are no longer interested in collectively creating something, then what's in store for America's future?" My mind is no longer on my workout as I leave the curl machine to begin tricep extensions. The well-known line from the movie, *Jerry McGuire*, "Show me the money," seemed to be turning into a way of life.

Had engaging in virtuous, creative enterprises taken a back seat to accumulating economic wealth? So many people seemed fixated on the idea of becoming a millionaire. They were trying to lasso the benefits of belonging to a club where America's affluent seemed to enjoy power, higher social status, and economic freedom.

Although there has always been a fascination with people of extraordinary wealth and power, there seems to be something different this time around. Yesterday's intrigue with marquee names such as Vanderbilt, Carnegie, and Rockefeller appeared to have given way to a fixation on how to become more like Bill Gates, Larry Ellison, and Warren Buffet. Also, a growing number of top-rated TV shows and bestselling books endorsed the theme of becoming a millionaire.

Everyone Wanted to Become the Next *Millionaire Next Door*

Who Wants to Be a Millionaire? quickly became our top-ranked TV show. Long gone were the days when shows like *The $25,000 Pyramid* offered what seemed to be an outrageous amount of money to keep us tuning in. Night after night, we religiously watched Regis Philbin and vicariously experienced the thrill of what it would be like to become an instant millionaire. Armed with the right answer to the final $1 million question, we each picture ourselves as being a gracious winner in front of a national audience.

In February 2000, we witnessed the marriage of two complete strangers on the *Who Wants to Marry a Multi-Millionaire?* TV show. That night, 22 million Americans watched a jazzed-up version of *The Dating Game* from the 1960s, as fifty attractive bachelorettes competed for the top spot. For her efforts, the winner received a $35,000, three-carat wedding ring, and an all-expenses-paid honeymoon on a Caribbean cruise with her new multi-millionaire husband. Yet, when the ship docked, the honeymoon was over. Simply put, they were "two people who could not get along in real life."

Three years later, "reality TV" would present 20 single women jetting off to France on Fox's *Joe Millionaire*. Each one had been duped into believing that the bachelor was a millionaire. And NBC's *For Love or Money* made it clear that a charming bachelor could not compete with $1 million dollars—the woman he erroneously chose for love picked the money instead.

At local convenience stores, people willingly stood in long lines and eagerly threw their hard-earned money away on an infinitessimal chance for the lottery's most recent jackpot. And why not? After all, somebody was eventually going to have that winning ticket and, in America, it could happen to you!

Then there were the day-traders who used options and margined accounts to place large bets on momentum stocks, trying to time the market's next direction. Still others put up with jobs they really didn't like so they could cash in on stock options. In more than a few cases, these people sacrificed their happiness, hoping their options would have significant value by the time they vested.

The majority of us, however, were intent on becoming affluent the old-fashioned way—sensibly over time—and we became students devoted to the process. We made books like *The Millionaire Next Door* and *Rich Dad, Poor Dad* runaway bestsellers. We tried to catch a glimpse of who the wealthy were and how they made it.

We also scoured magazines, trade publications, and other references for the keys to unlock the secrets of financial success. In October 1999, *Forbes* magazine put out an issue titled "The Billionaire Next Door." It revealed that of the then richest four-hundred Americans, more than half were billionaires!

A new classification of wealth appeared to be emerging. New-sprung definitions for affluence and social status were published in *Forbes* as follows:

	Income	Wealth
Superrich	$10 million+	$100 million+
Rich	$1-$10 million	$10 million-$100million
Upper-Middle	$75,000-$1 million	$500,000-$10 million
Middle	$35,000-$75,000	$55,000-$500,000
Lower-Middle	$15,000-$35,000	$10,000-$55,000
Poor	$0-$15,000	$0-$10,000

The stock market had been on a tear for nearly two decades, where the P/E (price-to-earnings ratio) quadrupled from 8 in 1980 to 32 in 1999. Other well-respected magazines like *The Wall Street Journal's Smart Money* and *Newsweek* captured the growing sentiment of what the American Dream had become for many. They adorned their respective covers with *"RETIRE TEN YEARS EARLY—It's America's newest obsession!"* and *"The whine of '99—everyone is getting rich but me."*

During the 1990s alone, the stock market increased by $10 trillion. Some people were making obscene amounts of money from new economy stocks, many of which did not have either profits or products.

Merrill Lynch's Henry Blodget was the most widely read analyst of the day. He needed only to predict that Amazon.com would have a price target of $400 someday, and Amazon stock would have been purchased by a lot of investors. Little did we know that Blodgett, in private, was scoffing to a select few about some of the very stocks he was recommending to the public. Most other analysts on Wall Street were bullish, too, and hardly a bear could be found. Prudential Securities' technical analyst, Ralph Acampora, as late as March 2000, was pounding the table with the misguided belief that the NASDAQ would hit the 6000 mark by the end of the year. Even the Federal Reserve Chairman, Alan Greenspan, reassured Congress, "Beneficent fundamentals will provide the framework for continued economic progress well into the new millennium."

Founders of Internet start-up companies, like Global Crossing's Chairman, Gary Winnick, made billions of dollars in a matter of months, whereas it took John D. Rockefeller 25 years to make his first billion. The brightest minds graduating from our universities were frantically developing business plans to secure venture-capital financing for new-economy companies to cash in on. Who had time to pursue a conventional MBA? In those days, two years seemed like a lifetime.

"Having" More Rather Than "Being" More

Underneath the shiny exterior of material gain, things just didn't seem to be quite right. A growing number of investors were counting on double-digit returns for the long-term and expecting to retire by the time they were 40. Still others, who were already retired, focused primarily on how to protect their financial wealth from unwarranted creditors and the obtrusive reach of Uncle Sam. As an advisor who routinely helped others achieve their material objectives, I found myself thinking of singer Peggy Lee's famous line, wondering "Is that all there is?"

I realized that advising people about money matters alone was neither comprehensive nor personally fulfilling. Perhaps I was too busy building a business made up of just "clients." I had let the financial focus of my profession get in the way of truly helping people plan wisely around their core-values. It became clear to me that many of us had lost touch with our heritage and the founding spirit that has made America a great nation.

Pope John Paul II best expressed my thoughts when he said, "It is not wrong to want to live better; what is wrong is a style of life presumed to be better when our actions are directed toward 'having' rather than 'being,' and which wants to have more, not in order to be more but in order to spend life in enjoyment as an end in itself."

"*The heartrending events of the last few years have changed our world and the way we view it. Nevertheless, they present us with windows of opportunity that we can use to uproot our complacency to begin anew. We just need to have the courage to act in accordance with the wisdom forged from difficult times.*"

—Charlie Douglas

Chapter 3

The Party Ends Badly as the Bubble Bursts

*"It is only natural for us to reach out for God,
country, and each other in times of great tragedy. Yet, our greatest
challenge going forward is to carry that selfless spirit as we
interact with each other in everyday life."*
—Charlie Douglas—

In some cases, the greed and envy that accompanied the chase for material gain were getting out of hand. During the late 1990s, it wasn't uncommon to read about a Wall Street analyst who had received an anonymous death threat from an enraged stockholder after he or she had downgraded a particular stock.

A few hundred yards from where I lived in Atlanta, a daytrader named Mark Barton, who had lost $105,000 in the stock market in a little over a month, and $500,000 altogether, went on a shooting spree. He left nine dead and thirteen wounded at several day-trading firms.

Barton was described as a typical nice guy who was always on the phone with his kids. Most likely, he was just an extreme example of someone who was emotionally unstable and snapped. On the other hand, a computer-generated suicide note found in Barton's apartment rationally touched upon the dark side of materialism—"I have come to hate this life in this system of things. I have come to have no hope."

Many of us were too busy enjoying the party to notice the telling signs of its coming demise. Some even took the party to new extremes. Ex-Tyco International's CEO, Dennis Kowalski, apparently used company funds to throw a million-dollar party for his wife on the Italian island of Sardinia. A memo from a Tyco employee detailed the festivities of the party: "The guests come into the pool area, the band is playing, they are dressed in elegant chic. Big ice sculpture of Michelangelo's David, lots of shellfish and caviar at his feet. A waiter is pouring Stoli vodka into the statue's back so it comes out its penis into a crystal glass."

The Bubble Bursts Under the Fed's Needle

The party ended badly in March 2002 as the bubble burst. Although it was not the Federal Reserve's job to burst the stock market's bubble, its policy of tightening short-term interest rates in 1999 and 2000 cannot be defended otherwise. Besides rising oil prices, there had been little or no evidence of inflation.

Why the Federal Reserve took no action to raise margin requirements (the amount of credit brokerage firms may extend customers for the purchase of securities—currently 50 percent), while raising short-term interest rates instead, is baffling. This is especially true given what Alan Greenspan said during a September 1996 meeting of the Fed's Open Market Committee: "I recognize there is a stock market bubble problem at this point;" he further asserted, "I guarantee if you want to get rid of the bubble, whatever it is, *increasing margin requirements* will do it."

Although raising margin requirements may not have ensured a steady deflation of the growing bubble, it would have at least sent a message to investors. Conjecturing whether irrational exuberance had unduly escalated asset values when the Dow Jones was at 6400 was not exactly decisive action. Unfortunately, raising short-term interest rates turned out the party's lights, and getting them back on has proven to be very difficult. The Fed even cut short-term interest rates over a dozen times since January 2001— to their lowest levels in 45 years—and yet the lights of solid economic recovery remained dim.

Our Financial World Has Changed

Today, my morning trips to the gym have noticeably changed. There are still a few loyal watchers of CNBC but Bartiromo's pre-market mantra is altogether different. During the past few years, she has begun many opening bells by telling us—"Well folks, technology and telecom shares are once again preparing to take it on the chin today." During the last few years, the S&P 500 was cut in half, and the once high-flying NASDAQ has twice been cut more than in half.

Altogether, the market at its 2002 low lost some $8.5 trillion—the worst bear market since the Great Depression. And high-priced market pundits like Goldman Sach's, Abby Joseph Cohen, a perennial bull, have lost a lot of credibility in recent years. Only in recent times, have stock analysts downgraded the very stocks and sectors that not long before that they said were strong buys.

As Wall Street prays that it has seen the bottom, for many it has been an agonizing time. I think of the cute voice of the seven year old who called about Lucent and was told it was a no-brainer as a long-term buy. In the fall of 2002, Lucent traded for under $1, having lost over 99 percent of its value. But Lucent has had a lot of company as a hungry bear has devoured many blue-chip stocks during its reign on Wall Street.

There have been far fewer green arrows along the ticker tape during the last couple of years, and many days it just looks like a sea of red. It is astounding how long it may take to earn money, and how quickly it can slip through your fingers. The guy on the treadmill next to me says, "Can't we watch something besides CNBC? For God's sake, this is a gym! You guys ever heard of ESPN?"

Creating Something May Require Us to Risk It All

A few people cashed out handsomely during the Internet's boom without creating anything at all. Others who had the courage to create something in the new economy were in some cases left empty-handed.

For example, eToys's founder and CEO, Toby Lenk, at one time was worth almost a $1 billion on paper. However, he wanted to create and run a respectable business, so he didn't sell any of his stock. Under Lenk's committed leadership, eToys became a profitable company and the third most-trafficked ecommerce website on the Internet.

Those impressive results meant little, however, to callous investment bankers who jumped ship when the Internet sector started heading south. Having relied on the promises of its financial backers, eToys was in the middle of a significant build-out and could not recover once investment bankers pulled the plug.

Toby lost all of his equity in eToys and walked away with only a modest salary after running the company for four years. Some said Lenk was foolish for not having taken most of his chips off the table far sooner, as many others in his situation had done. But I think Toby Lenk was rich in character—he endeavored to create something worth believing in.

In some key ways, Lenk was just like many Americans before him who risked everything for the dreams they believed in. Many successful entrepreneurs, like Wal-Mart founder Sam Walton, risked it all more than once. Even though they could have just cashed in, they continued forging ahead. They had bigger dreams and believed they could make a greater difference.

9/11 Was a Reality Check

I try to put Wall Street in perspective by thinking about the sobering events that occurred during the morning of September 11, 2001—the day the War Against Terrorism began. I often recall a piece from *USA Today* where American Airlines Flight 11, carrying ninety-two people, hit Tower One at 8:45 a.m. Minutes before the horrific impact, Norbert Pete, 42, had just made his first delivery.

As the building shook violently and a deafening explosion was still ringing in his ears, Pete, who was near a 79th-floor elevator, quickly pressed the down button. When the door opened, a blast of hot air and smoke shot out from the shaft. He thought of his seven-month-old son. "Okay, God, it's up to you and me now. You've got to help me get through this," he prayed as he headed for the stairs.

Brave firefighters made their way up congested stairs, hauling hoses and other heavy equipment. Upon seeing the firefighters, people began to cheer and applaud, not knowing these same men would all be dead in a matter of minutes. "Keep going down," the firefighters yelled as they marched up into the towering inferno. A woman remarks how good-looking they are—they are such fine young men.

Pete encounters the firefighters and offers to help. He makes his way to safety only after a commander thanks him and shouts, "Get the hell down the stairs!"

In the South Tower, Robert DeAngelis, an executive, started down from the 91st floor, but returned after hearing everything was okay. He called his wife, Denise, and told her that he did not believe what he was seeing—"My God, people are jumping from the windows of the North Tower." Denise screams on the other end of the line, "Robert, there is another plane coming! Get out of that building!" She watches helplessly as United Airlines Flight 175, carrying sixty-five people, slams into Tower Two at 9:03 a.m. near her husband's floor. The phone went dead.

It is hard to imagine choosing the way you will die—by a fire burning at more than 1,000 degrees or jumping from an unimaginable height. It is difficult to see a loving God in the course of the senseless loss of human life and great injustice. Perhaps there is comfort in remembering the selflessness of the crew and thirty-passengers of United Flight 93, which crashed in Shanksville, Pennsylvania that same day. They were all strangers who began a routine flight, yet some bound together with supernatural courage that began with the words, "Let's roll!"

The terrorists were deliberate in their chosen targets, and New York's Twin Towers stood out in particular. To the terrorists, they symbolized America's prideful arrogance of might and wealth in a world of economic disparity. To many of us, they represented the freedom of capitalism and a long line of Americans who dared to reach for a part of the American Dream.

But what struck me most about 9/11 was that Americans, all across the land, looked to God and their country for reassurance. For a time, people were markedly kinder to one another. Out of tragedy came a selflessness reminiscent of America's founding spirit.

We showed great compassion toward others. Many donated money, while others gave blood in the vain hope that more people would be found alive. We bought American flags everywhere they were sold and proudly displayed them from our homes and cars. America's leaders asked us to pray, and we responded like "One nation under God."

President George W. Bush addressed us from the Oval Office on the evening of 9/11 and said, "Tonight I ask for your prayers for all those who grieve, for the children whose worlds have been shattered, for all whose sense of safety and security have been threatened. And I pray that they will be comforted by a power greater than any of us, spoken of the ages in Psalm 23: 'Even though I walk through the valley of the shadow of death, I fear no evil for You are with me.'"

It is, however, only natural for us to reach out for God, country, and each other in times of great tragedy. Yet, our greatest challenge going forward is to carry that selfless spirit as we interact with each other in everyday life.

Our Ailing Institutions

As we looked hopefully to our nation's institutions for comfort after 9/11, we noticed that they had become weak from years of neglect. The moral sustenance they once provided had declined. Should we have been surprised? After all, we had mostly banned God from our public domain, and further distanced ourselves from the patriotic rituals that once bonded us all together as a nation.

After the terrorist attack, syndicated columnist Kathleen Parker recalled watching the memorial service at the National Cathedral on television. As the audience sang "The Battle Hymn of the Republic," she joined in from the back of the family room. It occurred to her that her son, as well as most American children, didn't know the words to that song or a half-dozen other patriotic tunes that are imprinted on older Americans' brains. In that moment, it dawned on her that many today have been and are being raised in godless institutions that have also lost touch with the importance of patriotism.

Virtues and values need to be continually nurtured if they are to be responsibly passed from one generation to the next. Parker writes, "If we are to win this war—sure to last into our children's futures—we have to reweave the rituals of God and country into our institutions. We can't expect our children to understand and defend a heritage they have never been given."

In our quest for material wealth, we have lost touch with our foundation and have misplaced meaningful values that used to help promote a sense of community and common identity. Today, although we continue to enjoy a level of personal independence and affluence unprecedented in America's history, it has come at a cost. There's been a decline in the integrity of our relationships with each other as well as with our Creator. According to a Gallup Poll completed the day before 9/11, 55 percent of the citizens of the wealthiest, most powerful nation in history were "dissatisfied with the way things were going in America."

To a large degree, we are living off the waning spiritual capital entrusted to us by previous generations. In the long-run, however, our institutions cannot thrive without the moralistic values and virtues on which they were created.

Let's Use 9/11 as a Wake-Up Call for a Better Future

The terrorist attack of 9/11 was certainly painful, but even more misfortune was soon to follow. Enron, the sixth largest company in America, shocked the nation as it scandalously imploded, and the biggest case of consumer fraud in American history occurred on Wall Street. Although September 11th was not able to dispel the emotions of greed and envy from occurring in some, it can serve as a wake-up call for all of us about the direction in which our nation may well be heading.

After a recent morning workout, I noticed a front-page story in *The Atlanta Journal-Constitution*. Ironically, it was about another day-trader named Fred Herder who had been wounded in Mark Barton's shooting spree of 1999. Herder, a retired chef, managed to survive Barton's onslaught. But a bullet was lodged in his back that the doctors never removed because it was too close to his spine.

In the article, Herder's ex-wife described him as a guy who didn't like to spend a lot. She said, "He never paid credit card interest; he researched cars for months before buying one; and he believed Christmas should be limited to only one nice gift."

Herder, who had been given a second chance at life, however, returned to day-trading at the very same firm he had sued for failing to provide adequate security during the Barton episode. Alas, within a matter of months, Herder's life ended in much the same way Barton's did. Herder's suicide email to his girlfriend read:

> My dear Shirley!
>
> As you know by now, my life came to an end and I lost in excess of $400,000 in the last three years. Most people who "day trade" lose money. I never had the necessary discipline, and most of the time I took on too much risk. Nobody else but myself is at fault. Certainly, I should have quit a long time ago when I still had some money left, but I was determined to make this work. I did not want to go back to the very stressful business world as an employee…. I could write a book about what went wrong in my life but that would not help you understand my action.

The heartrending events of the last few years have changed our world and the way we view it. Nevertheless, they present us with windows of opportunity that we can use to uproot our complacency to begin anew. We just need to have the courage to act in accordance with the wisdom forged from difficult times.

America is at a crossroad, and we need to choose wisely as we proceed. If we are to continue as a great nation and revitalize the American Dream, we need to reconnect with our country's founding spirit and our reason for being.

"There can only be two basic loves: the love of God unto the forgetfulness of self, or the love of self unto the forgetfulness and denial of God."**

—St. Augustine

Chapter 4

Our Reason for Being

"Jesus gave a daunting commandment—'Love others as I love you.'
But who among us today is willing to love our neighbor to the extent
of laying down our lives and possessions?"
—Charlie Douglas—

Throughout the course of history, man has looked to God and religion to answer fundamental questions regarding the human condition. Who am I? What is the purpose of life? Where can I find happiness? For most of the Christian era, people believed that God and salvation were humanity's primary concerns. What was accomplished and possessed during one's lifetime was secondary to living life in accordance with godly principles and virtues.

In recent times, however, many of us have been looking far less to God and religion to answer those fundamental questions. What we do for a living, consume, and possess essentially define people today. Psychoanalyst Eric Fromm observed of our modern era—"Today, life is strictly separated from religious values in that it is devoted to striving for material comforts, where man's happiness lies in the satisfaction of consuming."

God's Role v. God's Concerns

Today, many of us turn to God as a source for helping us achieve personal success. But how many turn to our Creator for the grace to live in accordance with selfless virtues? In some cases, our current view of God's role in our lives could lead us to ask a few more poignant questions.

Does God fret about how financially successful we can become? Or is our Creator more likely to be concerned that we often lack faith, and may not have enough love in our hearts for others? Should God be overly troubled if we don't retire 10 years earlier than we thought we could, because of a corporate downsizing or a brutal bear market? Or is it more likely that God may be offended by our materialistic actions if we make financial wealth our main goal, and seek happiness primarily from what we consume and possess?

In our efforts to answer those questions truthfully, many of us can't help but notice that the spiritual life we desire is inconsistent with the material world in which we live. Historian Arnold Toynbee observed, "...religious founders disagreed with each other in the pictures of what is the nature of the universe, the nature of spiritual life, the nature of ultimate reality. But they all agreed in their ethical precepts.... They all said with one voice that if we made material wealth our paramount aim, this would lead to disaster."

In our western culture, we are losing touch with the need to develop lasting wealth based on enduring virtues. Consider that in 1999, according to the United Nations Development Program, 26 percent of the world's people in high-income countries, such as the United States, consumed 86 percent of the world's goods.

The $8 billion annually that Americans spend on cosmetics could provide basic education to the world's poor—with $2 billion left over. The $11 billion Europeans spend on ice cream nearly equals the $12 billion cost of universal access to water and sanitation. Imagine what could be done for humanity with the hundreds of billions spent worldwide on cigarettes and alcohol. Sadly, the report concluded that it is not likely the world could arrive at an equitable distribution of goods and services.

In 2003, the United Nations Environment Program released a report that predicted more than half of humanity will be living with water shortages, depleted fisheries, and polluted coastlines within 50 years because of a worldwide water crisis. Over 90 percent of the severe problems are in developing nations, where they have poor irrigation and water supply practices due to impoverished economic conditions.

Does God really provide economic assistance to some while withholding it from others? Or do we need to take more responsibility for the economic inequality that exists in our world today?

A May 2000 edition of *USA Today* told a distressing story of an Ethiopian family. They were forced to leave their village because an unrelenting drought had nearly exhausted the stores of water and food. The family of five had to trek through 110-degree heat across a desert to reach a tiny settlement, where thousands of people clamored for the donated food being handed out by local officials.

During the journey, the family lost their one-year-old son on the first night, the three-year-old daughter the next day, and the two-year-old son that night. With each death, the family had little choice but to dig a simple hole, chant a prayer, and move on. When they reached the settlement, only the two parents and the donkey were still alive. They secured two bags of grain and began their three-day walk home—past the little mounds of their deceased children. The father, a very religious man, said only, "I suppose Allah thought their time had come." Was it really their time, or is this a painful example that in some way reflects humanity's unwillingness to share?

As the gap between those who have and those who do not widens, will our concept of God and the institution of religion ultimately become nothing more than tools used to bring about social order? Was Communist Karl Marx right in calling religion the "opiate for the masses"? We cannot afford to lose the sensitivity to our religious heritage.

Sigmund Freud, the father of psychoanalysis, believed that religion was nothing more than the projection of deep-seated wishes based on human need. Freud boldly predicted that as people become more educated, they would "turn away" from "the fairy tales of religion." But according to a recent Gallup Poll, even though more Americans are now better educated than ever, more also believe God plays a direct role in their lives.

Be that as it may, a roar of divisiveness is drowning out the indispensable values and virtues that religious institutions need to promote for the enrichment of all people. Christians separated from Judaism in the first century and never formed a meaningful relationship with Muslims, who established their faith in the eighth century. Thereafter, the Catholic Church saw the Orthodox leave in the twelfth century, while the Protestants left in the sixteenth. Jews and Muslims have been fighting over the "Promised Land" for thousands of years, with each faction confident that God is on their side. Since there is only one God, how can so many different faiths claim to have the truth?

God Is Love

The fact is that an overwhelming number of religions today, including all Christian religions, agree that God is love and we are His children. What separates us is found basically in the manner of expressing that common belief.

Philosopher Bernard Lonergan said, "All religious experience at its roots is an experience of an unconditional and unrestricted being in love." God is not some ethereal fatherly figure in the clouds, waiting to punish those who are naughty and reward those who are nice. God is the loving energy and unifying force of the universe that dwells within all living things. Our Creator is the source of all love from which we draw our supply. God loves divinely and unconditionally—not humanly and conditionally. The obvious virtue being extolled by God and religion is love. So what is love?

C.S. Lewis's *The Four Loves* offered four Greek words for love: *Storge*—affection for things and people; *Philia*—friendship or brotherly love; *Eros*—romantic love; and *Agape*—charity or Divine love.

Today, we love that special person who causes our heart to race. We are continually bombarded with romantic books like *The Bridges of Madison County,* romantic movies such as *When Harry Met Sally,* and love songs similar to Sinatra's "Strangers in the Night." All combine to help keep driving home the message that love is the magical feeling of affection.

More recently, ABC's *The Bachelor* and *The Bachelorette* help promote the notion that true love can somehow be manufactured through physical attraction and surreal dates with a flock of willing suitors. Some of us spend a lifetime searching for that special someone to arouse that feeling of passion or affection within us. Still others may end marital relationships, entered into under the promise of "until death do us part," primarily because that feeling is gone.

Aside from that romantic someone, we generally love our children, parents, siblings, pets, and a few close friends. In addition, we often love and have a strong affection for what we can buy and consume—we love big homes, new cars, stylish clothes, fine foods, exciting entertainment, and exotic vacations, to name but a few. Advertisers spend billions of dollars each year directly or indirectly telling us that if we buy their products or services, we will secure greater love for ourselves or others.

Selfless Love Is Easy Only in Theory

Rarely does the western world's definition of love mention the word God, nor does it imply that to love means to live with a charitable heart, where we act out of concern for others. Jesus gave us a daunting commandment—"Love others as I love you." But how many of us today love our neighbors to the extent of laying down our lives and possessions for them?

To love well is one of life's greatest challenges. With over 50 percent of marriages failing, it is obvious that many of us find it difficult to love even at home. Journalist G. K. Chesterton was right when he said, "It is not that Christianity hasn't been tried. It has been, and found difficult."

We must choose to act in unselfish ways out of concern for others. Love should not be based on how we feel since feelings can vary. Rather, love needs to come from our will which controls our actions. We would do well to incorporate the words of St. Augustine into our daily lives—"There can only be two basic loves: the love of God unto the forgetfulness of self, or the love of self unto the forgetfulness and denial of God."

"The lives of the super wealthy prove that money cannot buy love. Material wealth will never be able to satisfy the longing of the human soul. But material wealth gives those who have it a broader array of choices and a greater power to effect positive change—provided they choose wisely."

—Charlie Douglas

Chapter 5

Money Can't Buy Me Love

"More than any money we may acquire, it's the
spiritual capital we dispense and our concern for others that
ultimately determines whether we have lived a rich life."
—Charlie Douglas—

In the 1960s, the Beatles sang the number-one song, "Money Can't Buy Me Love." The song embodied the simple truth that just because you have money doesn't mean you can buy love. For those who have attained financial wealth, has their ability to love been enhanced or hindered in the process of acquiring and possessing riches? To help answer that question, let's take a brief look at a few of America's wealthiest individuals whose stories have withstood the test of time.

Legacies of Great Possessions With Little Love Passed On

The first three financially rich individuals were truly exceptional businesspeople. Each, in that person's time, was the richest of his or her gender in America. Sadly, however, they all left undersized legacies of love.

Cornelius Vanderbilt was the wealthiest industrialist of the Gilded Age. He accumulated extraordinary financial wealth by providing transportation. His first fortune was ultimately built with the steamboats that handled roughly 75 percent of America's commerce as they traveled through New York's harbors. His next fortune was made by investing in railroad stocks and consolidating New York's rail lines.

Like other successful businessmen of that era, he was tough and often took matters into his own hands. Vanderbilt once said, "My God, you don't suppose you can run a railroad in accordance with the statutes of New York." On another occasion, he told a troublesome competitor, "I won't sue you for the law is too slow. I'll ruin you!"

Mark Twain wrote to Vanderbilt, who was never known for his philanthropy, and recommended that he do one worthy act before it was too late. Yet, it was due mainly to the insistence of his second wife, a 33-year-old cousin from Alabama, that Vanderbilt, shortly before his death, gave $1 million to a small southern college that was renamed after him.

At his death in 1877, he was the richest man in America with an estate worth more than $100 million—more money than there was in the U.S. Treasury. He left no money to charity, paid no estate taxes, and despite having thirteen children, he bequeathed 90 percent of his estate to his eldest son, William Henry. Remarkably, the son doubled the family fortune within seven years.

Vanderbilt's deathbed wish was "Keep the money together and keep the New York Central our road." Yet the Vanderbilt empire was dramatically weakened over the next two generations due to lavish spending, family lawsuits, and subdivisions among grudging heirs.

In the end, the Vanderbilts were unable to keep the money together, and they lost the New York Central. And when eldest son William Henry was asked by a reporter whether the railroads should be run for the public benefit, he replied, "The public be damned." At that point, the Vanderbilts lost a lot of the public's admiration as well. Less than 100 years after Cornelius's death, not even one of his 120 descendents, who gathered at Vanderbilt University in 1973 for the first family reunion, was a millionaire.

Hetty Green was the richest woman in America and perhaps one of the most detested too. Known as the "Witch of Wall Street," she became a player in the financial markets at a time when Wall Street was for men only.

She remarkably turned a $1 million inheritance into $100 million. Her investment philosophy was simple, yet potent, "I don't much believe in stocks. I never buy industrials. Railroads and real estate are the things I like. Before deciding on an investment, I seek out every kind of information about it. There is no secret in fortune making. All you have to do is buy cheap and sell dear, act with thrift and shrewdness and be persistent."

Although Hetty was in many ways a financial genius, she was also an unscrupulous and uncompassionate businesswoman. But most of all, she was an implausible miser. On one occasion, she spent half the night looking for a two-cent stamp that had fallen off a letter. On another, she carelessly took a crowded street car to make an enormous deposit in bearer bonds. When her bankers questioned her on why she took such a risk and didn't, instead, take a private carriage, she responded, "A carriage indeed! Perhaps you can afford to ride in a carriage but I cannot."

Spending a great deal of time on Wall Street and elsewhere in New York, Hetty did everything she could to avoid being considered a resident there since she did not want to be subject to taxation there. She resorted to staying in rooming houses and cheap hotels, and often used an empty desk at her bank as her office. Perhaps the most pitiful example of her tightwad manner was when she refused to seek medical attention for her son's leg since she believed that seeing a doctor would be too expensive. Regrettably, her son had to have his leg amputated.

Had there been a *Forbes 400* when she died, she would have easily been within the top twenty. Nevertheless, her millions had largely been stockpiled away where they simply collected interest and accumulated dust. Although she left no money to charity, her legacy has not been forgotten. She remains in the *Guinness Book of World Records*, listed as the "Most Miserly Woman in the World."

When **John Paul Getty** discovered the largest oil reserve in the world in Saudi Arabia, he established himself as the world's richest man. Yet, for Getty and his family, his money brought greater problems than it could solve.

For most of his life, Getty remained virtually unknown to the public; however, that changed at age 64 when a Paris gossip columnist leaked to *Time* magazine word of Getty's inordinate wealth. As Getty became better known to the public, the word *cheapskate* did not quite do justice for some who encountered him. For example, if you wanted to make a call from his home, you had to use a pay phone. If you stayed for dinner, he determined your worth beforehand and served you accordingly.

He paid only an offensive $1,200 a month for six months to the man who discovered the largest oil reserve in the world, and then cut him off. Moreover, for a long time, he refused to pay the ransom to his grandson's kidnappers, the Italian Mafia, even after they sent the grandson's bloodied ear in the mail to show they meant business. When Getty finally acquiesced, he loaned his son $1 million dollars as a part of the ransom price, charging the son interest.

Getty was married and divorced five times. Of his four sons who reached adulthood, only one survived relatively unharmed. One committed suicide, and one became a drug-addicted recluse before eventually finding new life in philanthropy. The third had to bear the life-long stigma of being disinherited in childhood because his mother had negotiated such a tough divorce with Getty.

When he died, Getty left a mere pittance for twelve women who had befriended him, each one believing she would be the lucky one to receive a ticket to a life of luxury. Instead, the bulk of Getty's remaining estate was left as a memorial to himself in the form of a bequest to the Getty Trust, the centerpiece of which is the Getty Museum.

During the construction of the world's richest museum, Getty even refused to pay for the museum director's electric pencil sharpener, threatening to fire him for such extravagance. Aside from helping to expand the world of art and humanities, Getty's legacy is rooted, above all, in oil and the money it produced. Unfortunately, his billions brought little in the way of love to others or himself.

Selfless Philanthropy or Selfish Promotion?

Our next two examples of extraordinary financial wealth were from the same era, and they are, perhaps, America's most noted philanthropists. They had tarnished images, but even so, humanity still owes them a great debt of gratitude for their generosity. It will forever be debated how much of their philanthropy was done out of love, and how much was well-timed and self-advertised to improve the public's perception of them.

Andrew Carnegie fought his way out of the slums of Pittsburgh to amass a great financial fortune. He invested in rail cars, telegraph communications, oil, and steel bridges. At 33, he was worth $400,000 (nearly $5 million in today's dollars) and had a guaranteed annual income of $50,000 (nearly $600,000 in today's dollars). Nevertheless, he was troubled by his wealth and wrote a letter to himself promising that he would stop working in two years and pursue a life devoted to education, writing, and philanthropy—"To continue much longer overwhelmed by business cares...must degrade me beyond hope of permanent recovery." Yet like many others of great financial wealth, Carnegie did not leave the game when his two years were up.

In many ways, Carnegie was a Jekyll and Hyde. On one hand, he amassed a fortune by crushing his competitors and exploiting his workers. He paid his steelworkers a miserly $2.50 a day for working twelve hours a day, seven days a week. He also used drastic methods to break unions when his workers united to strike against intolerable working conditions. On the other hand, he championed philanthropy by giving away the vast bulk of his wealth.

Carnegie, an atheist, nevertheless espoused some impressive views on philanthropy in *The North American Review* in 1889 in an article titled, "The Gospel of Wealth." Carnegie viewed the accumulation of wealth in the hands of a few as a very good thing. He was a Social Darwinist who believed in natural selection and survival of the fittest. On the other hand, Carnegie also believed that a man of great wealth should "become the sole agent and trustee for his poorer brethren, bringing to their service his superior wisdom, experience, and the ability to administer—doing for them better than they would or could do for themselves."

Carnegie was adamantly opposed to leaving wealth to family members—even to the first son—as was common practice at the time. He stated that "great sums bequeathed more often work for the injury than for the good of the recipients." He added, "The parent who leaves his son enormous wealth generally deadens the talents and energies of the son and tempts him to lead a less useful and less worthy life than he would otherwise."

Carnegie further said, "A rich man who dies rich dies in disgrace." Therefore, he was very much against waiting until death to leave wealth for public uses. He believed that the community, in the form of the state, should not be deprived its proper share. He felt that by taxing estates heavily at death, the state marks its condemnation of the selfish millionaire's unworthy life.

When he sold Carnegie Steel to J.P. Morgan in 1901, for about $400 million, Carnegie was the richest man in the world. Yet, by the time of his death in 1919, he had given away over $350 million to public causes. In all, Carnegie made good on his word and gave away roughly 90 percent of his fortune during his lifetime.

John D. Rockefeller became the richest man in the world and its first billionaire. Through his company, Standard Oil, Rockefeller, for a time, controlled over 90 percent of the oil-refining industry. He sincerely believed God had given him his money and that the power to make money was a gift from God. In particular, Rockefeller saw it as his duty to make money, and still more money—and to use the money he earned for the good of his fellow man.

He was impressed by Andrew Carnegie's *The Gospel of Wealth* and personally wrote Carnegie—"I would that more men of wealth were doing as you are with your money, but be assured your example will bear fruits, and the time will come when men of wealth will more generally be willing to use it for the good of others."

Rockefeller, a devoted Baptist, likewise became an outstanding philanthropist, giving away more than $500 million to charitable endeavors before he died. The Rockefeller Foundation was established to "promote the well-being of mankind throughout the world" and was initially funded with $250 million. Today, it has a market value in excess of $3 billion and has given more than $2 billion to grantees worldwide.

But Rockefeller was often unscrupulous in his business practices, leading Senator Robert LaFollete to call him "the greatest criminal of the age." Cartoonists often portrayed Rockefeller as a hypocrite who would give away coins with one hand and steal bags of gold with the other. He frequently received kickbacks and drawbacks as he forced railroads to pay him a portion of the shipping fees they collected from his competitors. Furthermore, as he continued to increase market share within the oil-refining industry, he offered his competitors a simple choice—either receive stock in Standard Oil in exchange for their businesses, or be put out of business.

Teddy Roosevelt viewed Rockefeller as the worst of the "malefactors of great wealth" and used the Sherman Antitrust Act to break up Standard Oil. Ironically, this served only to bring Rockefeller even greater riches as he was still part owner of the 34 companies that Standard Oil was broken into.

Before he died, and to avoid estate taxes, Rockefeller gave his son, John D. Rockefeller Jr., virtually all of his remaining fortune—close to $500 million. Junior, who had earlier suffered a nervous breakdown working in his father's business, spent the rest of his life in the role of the good steward. With philanthropic integrity, he did his best to dispense the money his father had, in some cases, callously made.

Two Legacies Rich in Financial and Spiritual Capital

The next two well-to-do businessmen were of great character and integrity. They made their mark not only by the tremendous financial wealth they amassed, but even more so by the love they passed on to others.

J.C. Penney was reared to believe that life was to be lived in accordance with the Golden Rule (Luke 6:31)—"Do unto others as you would have them do unto you." Good intentions, however, did not always meet with good results. Penney failed at his first business when he lost a major account simply because he refused to throw in a bottle of whiskey as a premium. For his principled conduct, Penney lost his business and all that he had saved.

Prophetically, Penney next worked for the Golden Rule Store, which he eventually bought and renamed after himself. His dream was to provide low-priced quality goods all over America. To help him reach his dream, he brought in thousands of junior partners.

All were handpicked by J.C. himself and, foremost, they were men of integrity.

All during his life, Penney relied heavily on his faith for strength as he had his share of troubles. His wife died when he was just 35, leaving him a widower with two children. For a time, Penney battled against thoughts of suicide.

His troubles continued when, in 1929, he pledged a large amount of Penney's stock, then worth $40 million, as collateral to get bank loans. The loans were not used to run his business but, instead, to further charitable endeavors at Penney farms. The farms essentially allowed the economically disadvantaged to have land of their own if they committed to working it for one year.

Unfortunately, during the Depression, Penney stock went from $120 to $13, and J.C. lost everything. He was broke at age 56 and checked into a mental hospital. But, in time, his faith and a recovering economy provided a way for him to recapture his peace of mind and financial wealth.

As the world of retail modernized and competition intensified, J.C. Penney was still unwilling to compromise his values. In the 1950s, when credit cards were first introduced, they were an instant boon to retailers as people could buy now and pay later. Penney, however, was against the use of credit cards and held firm on his cash-only policy until he was outvoted by the board. Penney's reasoning against allowing customers to use credit cards was simply that he thought it would result in people being oversold. And that was not in keeping with the Golden Rule.

Milton Hershey became the real-life Willy Wonka of the chocolate factory that bore his name. En route to becoming the chocolate king, however, he failed at his first two businesses. His relatives, who had earlier been willing to support him, now refused to take him in. Hershey, though, had a unique ability to rise up from failure. He lived in a time where chocolate was available only to the wealthy, but his dream was to make quality chocolate affordable to the masses. He believed that if you gave people quality, it was the best advertising and surest way to succeed.

Hershey used the proceeds from the sale of a caramel business to build a chocolate factory in Hershey, Pennsylvania. But he built much more than just a factory. Like the care he put into making chocolate, he had quality homes constructed for his workers and developed a model planned community. A bank, department store, school, park, churches, golf courses, zoo, and even a trolley system to carry workers were all built in rapid succession. Likewise, his home, which was modest for a man of his means, was built near the factory.

While other businessmen were trying to survive the Depression, Hershey hired workers and expanded his business. Even though the community of Hershey had been well-established for years, he started a second building boom during the Depression. He kept men at work constructing a grand hotel, a community building, a sports arena, and a new office building for the chocolate factory. When the strikes that took place against nearly all industrialists eventually found their way to the Hershey factory, they were very short-lived because of Hershey's character. His ceaseless labor and concern for others were an inspiration to all who worked for him.

Hershey, who had a strong religious upbringing, believed that an individual is morally obligated to share the fruits of his or her labor. Deeply saddened that he and his wife had no children of their own, Hershey founded a school for orphans—the Milton Hershey School. It was the pride of his life and received the bulk of his $60 million estate. Today, the 10,000-acre school houses and provides education for over a thousand children whose family lives have been disrupted. Hershey's personal convictions regarding wealth, his company, and the town he founded have, like his chocolates, been sweet experiences for many.

Today's Rich and the Legacies They Plan to Leave

What about some of today's richest people and their views on wealth? **Bill Gates**, the world's richest man, has said that he would give each of his children $10 million and donate the rest to charity. He thinks that too much inherited wealth is detrimental to one's well-being.

Regarding charity, Gates and his wife, Melinda, have established the world's largest private foundation and funded it with $17 billion. Among other things, the foundation focuses on improving health in the world's most vulnerable populations, equipping libraries in poorer communities with computers, and offering scholarships for ethnic and racial groups that are currently underrepresented in higher education.

Investment magnate **Warren Buffet** has also voiced concern over the potential negative impact of his sizable estate on his children's work efforts. Like an investor who has accumulated his wealth looking for value, Buffet also believes a child's development would not be facilitated by letting him or her start a 100-yard dash at the 50-yard line. Therefore, he and his wife are reportedly planning to give away 98 percent of their estate to the Buffet Foundation, as well as to other charities. Buffet's philosophy is simple—"Give enough money to your kids so they can do anything, but not enough so they can do nothing."

Our Greatest Challenge

The lives of the super wealthy prove that money cannot buy love. Material wealth will never be able to satisfy the longing of the human soul. But material wealth does give those who have it a broader array of choices and a greater power to effect positive change—provided they choose wisely.

More than any amount of money we may acquire, though, it's the spiritual capital we dispense and our concern for others that ultimately determines whether we have lived a rich life. But the biggest obstacle we face has nothing to do with money or what it can or cannot buy. Our greatest challenge is to love others.

"**A** person finds identity only to the extent that he commits to something beyond himself, to a cause greater than himself."

—Victor Frankl

Chapter 6

We Are Not Born Loving

*"We may spend our entire lives learning how to
grow in love while dealing with an ego that continually says,
'Hey, world, stop and look at me.'"*
—Charlie Douglas—

We are created in the image of a loving God, but we are not born loving. We are born narcissistic. Babies demand that their own wants and needs be satisfied first. They want to be held, fed, burped, changed, and entertained on demand.

As we get a little older, we want to play with and not share our toys, stay up as late as we want to, and eat as many sugar-filled snacks as we like. But mostly, we want to be the center of our parents' attention and have their world revolve around us. As we move into adulthood, many of us carry that need for special attention and recognition into our families, communities, and workplaces.

Learning to Love and Our Capacity for Love

The ability to respect ourselves and love others needs to be taught and nurtured through effective role modeling, instruction, and encouragement. It is preferably from our institutions, starting with our family of origin, that we begin to learn that love, among other things, is sharing, commitment, forgiveness, and treating others compassionately.

As we move from adolescence into adulthood, we become more affected by other institutional forces, such as religion, school, business, and government—each one playing a role in the development of our values. We may spend our entire lives learning how to grow in love, while dealing with an ego that continually says, "Hey, world, stop and look at me."

At the same time, we are created with a tremendous capacity to love. A few standouts like Ghandi and Mother Teresa managed to make remarkable progress at love and have exemplified our potential for it. They extended their acts of kindness beyond family members, close friends, and the so-called "desirable" people in society. They included unwanted strangers and even foes.

Ghandi and Mother Teresa were so successful at producing love because they practiced it tirelessly. They did not withhold love, saving it for a particular group. Rather, they helped Hindus become better Hindus, Muslims become better Muslims, and Christians become better Christians. As Gandhi said of love as it relates to Christianity—"If Christians were to live their Christian lives to the fullest, there would not be one Hindu left in India."

EGO Means—*Edge God Out*

What keeps many of us from realizing our potential to generate love? Frequently, it is our ego—that childish voice that we carry within that is intent on convincing us of the way things should be. The ego stresses self-importance and wants to boast, judge, and condemn.

It is our ego that gets attached to ideals and notions of justice and fairness. It covets and gets jealous as it wants to be rewarded and remembered. The ego believes that we are what we do, what we have, and what others think of us. Therefore, the ego needs to be special and stand apart. It continually looks up and down but never at the same level. It has to have the right physical attributes, degrees, and possessions to be on top.

The ego erroneously believes that more is better. It prevents us from understanding that if we are not grateful for what we have in our lives today, we probably won't be content with what we get tomorrow. When we allow the ego to be in charge, we never seem to achieve enough to keep it satisfied for long. The novelty of whatever we've accomplished or acquired wears off time and time again. Life is a journey, and the station that says

"We have arrived for good," constantly outdistances the train we are riding.

The worst part of the ego, however, is that it can prevent us from connecting with God and the Divine voice within. The ego is often like a thick layer of clouds that keeps us from experiencing blue skies and the warmth of the sun. Although God, like blue skies, is always there, the ego edges God right out of the picture.

Love, Marriage, and Children

Many of us begin to understand what love is only when we marry that special someone and give up the freedoms of being single. We discover that love is more than an affectionate feeling as we learn about commitment, forgiveness, and consideration of another person's wants and needs. No longer able to just do what solely pleases us, we need to search for things in common with our spouse and make reasonable compromises. Once we are married, what we do, how we spend or invest our money, and with whom we share our time all change in many ways.

Bring children into the picture and we give up even more of our freedom. Yet, despite the inconveniences, both marriage and children can bring us some of life's most joyful and fulfilling experiences. It is ironic that the loss of some of our personal freedom as a result of these commitments is what frees us to experience love. In fact, it is through commitment and concern for others that we encounter love and find our purpose. Victor Frankl said, "A person finds identity only to the extent that he commits to something beyond himself, to a cause greater than himself."

But is it possible to balance lives of fulfilling careers and material wealth with happy marriages and well-adjusted children? Or do we deceive ourselves by trying to serve too many masters?

I once traveled to the Greek Isle of Rhodes and met a local woman who did not allow her children to play with battery-operated or electrical toys. I thought to myself, "How do these kids get through the day without Pokemon™ or Gameboy™?" This woman explained that she wanted them to use their imaginations and develop their ingenuity with "old fashioned toys." I asked if it bothered her to deprive the children of some of the modern toys like Microsoft's Xbox™ that most other kids played with. She responded unequivocally "No!"

Her philosophy was simple enough—"We provide food and shelter for our children, and they do not want for any necessities. But most of all, we spend a lot of quality time with our children and give them love. We think they are very rich!"

Are our children today being given the love and attention they need? Mother Teresa offered the following opinion—"Children have lost their place in the family. Children are very, very lonely! When children come home from school, there is no one to greet them. Then they go back to the streets. We must find our children and bring them back home.

"Mothers are at the heart of the family. If the mothers are there, the children will be there too. Everybody today seems to be in such a terrible rush, anxious for greater development and greater riches. Children have very little time for their parents, and parents have very little time for their children and each other. So the breakdown of peace in the world begins at home."

We Need to Be on a Mission to Love Others

What will become of us and the American Dream if we continue down a materialistic road that increasingly distances itself from God, virtues, and the development of spiritual capital? What will be the fate of our nation should we reach the point where we no longer see others as part of ourselves? If we lose touch with our mission to love, we will be left with only our narcissistic selves. And history has shown, time and time again, that unchecked narcissism inevitably leads to a society's downfall.

Long before any fallen society began to experience the effects of an external breakdown, there was first a gradual but deadly decay of love-centered values. Our pursuit of materialism may lead to the degeneration of our nation, much like years of improper oral hygiene result in the deterioration of teeth and gums.

Will we have to endure the tormenting lessons that the ancient Israelites experienced over and over again? Every time the Israelites focused on things that took them away from God and toward idols, they suffered terrible hardship. Today it appears that America may be falling into the same trap; only now the golden calf is the almighty dollar.

More than 200 years ago, a professor named Alexander Tytler wrote, "The average age of the world's greatest civilizations has been only 200 years." Moreover, Tytler pointed out that these civilizations all passed through similar cycles "...from bondage to spiritual faith, to great courage, to abundance, to selfishness, to apathy, to dependency, and back to bondage," where the cycle begins again. Could it be that America is running on borrowed time?

If we are to revitalize the American Dream, we need to look at our past and determine how we can live a better tomorrow. Therefore, it is important to revisit the inception of the Dream as it was being experienced when America was first colonized. Likewise, it is essential to reexamine the crucial role that our institutional environment played in shaping the heritage entrusted to today's Retirees, Baby Boomers, and Generation Xers, as the Dream was passed on from one generation to the next.

Though categorizing people into particular generations and making broad generalizations has limitations, it is fairly indicative of our changing values and the direction in which we are heading. As Winston Churchill said, "The farther backward you look the farther forward you'll be able to see."

"When these spirit-filled colonists first set foot on shore of the New World, they were full of hope. Far from saints, their religious virtues, nevertheless, instilled in them the willingness to be productive, to graciously share their blessings, and to reinvest the fruits of their labors—to live each day planting the seeds of spiritual capital."

—Charlie Douglas

Chapter 7

The Rise of the Protestant Work Ethic

*"Protestants believed they were called by God to use
their unique gifts and talents in creative enterprise for the glory of God.
Made in the image of their Creator, they envisioned themselves to be
co-creators with a vocation to develop the New World."*
—Charlie Douglas—

Amerca is the financial capital of the world—the wealthiest nation on the planet. We have experienced tremendous prosperity since our humble beginnings a little over 200 years ago. Why?

Our prosperity can be explained, in part, by a society devoted to capitalism and the technological advancements of the Industrial Revolution. Capitalism, however, was born out of European philosophical thought, and the Industrial Revolution was confined largely to Britain. These catalysts of development were more readily available to other parts of the world and could have been better exploited by other nations who were wealthier than America at the time. So why did capitalism blossom in America?

Unique to America was the combination of industrialism, capitalism, and limited government, all of which were energized by the resourceful spirit of the Protestant work ethic. Americans had a lot of incentive to build the greatest, freest country in the world, and they weren't afraid to work for it.

The Role of the Catholic Church Prior to Protestantism

Before the sixteenth century, Protestants didn't exist. Instead, today's oldest and largest Christian institution, the Catholic Church, dramatically influenced the spiritual and temporal affairs of Western civilization. This occurred beginning in the fourth century, after the fall of the Roman Empire, primarily because the Church was the largest and most stable institution left standing. It simply expanded its role to fill the power vacuum that had been formed.

For many centuries under the Church's guidance, economies were stable but grew very slowly. Most people worked as necessary to support only their immediate needs. Like the ancient Greeks before them, work was often seen by higher social classes as an activity to be avoided and left instead to serfs and peasants. Aristocratic wealth was rooted in land and inherited wealth, but society frowned upon wealth that was earned through commerce or manufacturing. Frequently, the best and brightest became priests and part of the Church's growing bureaucracy. At the same time, the Church was increasingly composed of those who were often better skilled as politicians and lawyers than trained theologians.

Over the centuries, the Church dramatically increased its power base and became an integral part of governing states throughout Western Europe. It held a significant role in formulating the political policy that was ultimately carried out by the state. Toward the end of the eleventh century, Pope Gregory VII recognized the potential pitfalls of this fusion between Church and State and tried to separate the two, making distinct the spiritual and temporal powers in the Episcopal office. But he was strongly opposed and died in exile.

In some ways, the Church had grown too powerful and had become too entrenched in states' affairs, making some of its leaders vulnerable to the corruption that misuse of power often brings. Once power is obtained, it is not easy to use it wisely or to relinquish it—not even for an institution dedicated to carrying out the divine mission of spreading God's love.

The Most Important Religious Event to Affect America

In the early part of the sixteenth century, the most important religious event to ever affect America took place. The Protestant Reformation began when a Catholic priest named Martin Luther openly challenged questionable practices by some within the Catholic Church.

Luther, however, had no intention of founding a new church. He thought that by openly challenging the Catholic Church to return to the Bible alone, the Church would reform itself, including abandoning many of its Sacraments and long-held traditions. Luther miscalculated and was excommunicated.

One of the most far-reaching technological developments ever invented greatly aided the rise of Protestantism. Johannes Gutenberg's printing press of 1450 allowed the Bible to become available to the masses. This greatly shifted power away from the dominant Catholic Church and empowered the individual Christian.

Many Christians could now directly relate to God through their own Bible and no longer believed that they needed to proceed through the Catholic Church. This also allowed the Bible to be individually interpreted and, today, has resulted in a multitude of Protestant faiths and sects that attempt to explain the Bible from a variety of perspectives.

Pursue the Kingdom of God and Live Simply

Luther proclaimed the idea that God calls us to specific tasks. He set forth the notion that in answering your calling you were to work hard and dedicate yourself to it—thereby giving glory to God by succeeding at your work.

Luther believed that people should always fill their lives with useful and sober occupations suitable for their states of existence. Believers were sanctioned to choose the employment or vocation in which they were to be most serviceable to God, not merely to themselves or for their own economic well-being.

Economically, Luther interpreted the scriptures as a call to live very simply and, like Catholics, to address just one's basic needs. Material goods were to be used and accumulated only to sustain life and serve the Kingdom of God.

Luther was hardly a capitalist and believed that interest should be prohibited from being earned when money was loaned. Furthermore, he professed that a man should only sell his goods for a fair price, even if the market could command a much higher one.

The long-held theological belief endorsed by Luther and the Catholic Church was that man was to be dependent upon God for all things, including his essential material needs. It was a biblical principle found in Luke 12:31 and Matthew 6:33 that God would continue to provide the basic necessities of life for those who pursued the Kingdom of God above all else.

Although Luther's message was spiritually compelling, it was difficult for emancipated men of the Renaissance to embrace commercially. The Renaissance, which led into the Reformation, was a period of great cultural renewal during which art, literature, science, philosophy, and economics soared to new heights.

The Role of Profit in Salvation

It has been said that "when the student is ready the teacher will arrive." Likewise, when an economic environment changes substantially, new leaders with fresh ideals often will emerge to accommodate the transformation. During the material and tech-nological progress of the Renaissance, it was becoming increasingly difficult to reconcile a spirituality that was rooted in the poverty of the gospels. At that time, almost 16 centuries of theology became financially modernized.

John Calvin, a French lawyer, turned theology upside down by bringing the gospel into the newly transformed world of the Renaissance. Calvin was the first to promote a theological basis for materialism that was adopted by the masses. Whereas Luther taught it was sinful to accumulate money beyond what was necessary for subsistence, Calvin helped sow the seeds of capitalism by proclaiming that profit was now to be seen as a grace from God.

Theologically, Calvin believed in predestination and that most would be damned; however, God saves those select few whom He has chosen. But how was one to know whether or not he or she was saved? The answer for Calvin was that although good works were useless as a means of attaining salvation, they were indispensable as a sign of election.

Calvinists used good works as evidence to persuade them-selves and others that they were predestined for eternal life.

Success at one's work or calling was proof that one was living a well-ordered, disciplined life and would be saved.

Under Calvin, there was a great commitment to earning, producing, and saving, rather than consuming. This belief greatly encouraged the accumulation of capital for investment and business expansion. Moreover, Calvin had a liberal view of commerce and banking, and endorsed lending money with interest. Therefore, it was now permissible to develop business and commerce through debt, without spiritual condemnation.

Calvinism had one major drawback—wealth was considered bad if used for personal enjoyment. Although you pursued material success as a sign of election, you could not enjoy the fruits of your labors, especially luxuries. You were to affably share some of your profits with the community, and reinvest the remainder in your calling, which in turn served to increase profitability.

As Max Weber stated in *The Protestant Ethic and The Spirit of Capitalism*—"To be idle, let alone relaxing, was to be sinful and guilty of sloth. Even the wealthy were not to eat without working. For although they did not need to labor to support their own needs, there was God's commandment that they, like the poor, must obey. For everyone had prepared a calling, which he should profess and in which he should labor. This calling was God's commandment to the individual to work for the divine glory."

America's Religious Mindset

It was with this mindset that the Puritans, who were themselves Calvinists, set sail in the 1630s. Back in England, they had hoped to "purify" the Church of England of some of its Roman Catholic attributes, but they soon fled to the New World under persecution from King Charles.

The Puritans had been people of economic means and political influence while in England, and they soon became the most dynamic force in the American colonies, affecting other Protestant beliefs. In due course, capitalism took hold with its private ownership, free markets, and incentive for profit. It flourished here especially because many Protestants believed they were called by

God to use their unique gifts and talents in creative enterprise for the glory of God. Made in the image of their Creator, they envisioned themselves to be co-creators with a vocation to develop the New World.

When these spirit-filled colonists first set foot on the shores of the New World, they were full of hope. Far from saints, their religious virtues, nevertheless, instilled in them the willingness to be productive, to graciously share their blessings, and to reinvest the fruits of their labors—to live each day planting the seeds of spiritual capital.

In the course of time, however, Calvin's forbidden fruits lured many into an insatiable appetite for consumption and material comfort. Evidently, the Protestant work ethic offered little protection against the material temptation that has beset humanity ever since the time of Adam and Eve.

"*Americans' chief business is to secure for themselves a government which allows them to acquire the things they covet, and which will not debar them from the peaceful enjoyment of those possessions which they have already acquired.*"

—Alexis de Tocqueville

Chapter 8

The Price Paid for Capitalism

*"Americans indulged themselves one too many times
with instant gratification and conspicuous consumption."*
—Charlie Douglas—

W
e don't get out of shape in one day, which is as true of being spiritually grounded as it is of being physically fit. But as visits to the gym or quiet time for prayer and charitable endeavors become less frequent, there comes a day when we wake up and notice we are terribly out of shape.

We wonder how in the world we let ourselves get that way because only now does the unsightliness of our present condition seem obvious. Likewise, the seduction of consumerism developed slowly in America, taking three steps forward then two back. As the years progressed, we became fat around the middle and lost sight of our foundational spiritual fitness.

The Stock Market Finds a Home on Wall Street

Before our first President, George Washington, voluntarily left office, he appointed Alexander Hamilton as Secretary of the Treasury. Hamilton's appointment was significant because he transformed our country's credit system and gave Wall Street its start as a securities market. In accordance with Hamilton's plan, we began trading bonds to refund the debt incurred during the Revolutionary War.

The securities markets eventually found a home on Wall Street in New York City, rather than the more financially established Philadelphia. This occurred primarily because of the eruption in commerce that came to New York as a result of the completion of the Erie Canal. New York quickly became the biggest boomtown the modern world has ever known. As the city expanded, Manhattan Island, which is only about two miles wide, became incredibly valuable real estate.

John Jacob Astor, who had amassed a fortune with the largest fur-trading business in America, sold his company and, at age 71, bought as much Manhattan real estate as he could afford. He owned a particularly large chunk of the desolate northern part of Manhattan and gambled that the growing city would eventually expand there. His gamble paid off handsomely. He bought in acres and sold in lots, and became Manhattan's largest landowner.

As the "Landlord of New York," he had the means to do much for society but, like a growing number of capitalists at that time, he was not charitably inclined. When he died in 1848, his estate was worth $20 million, making him the richest man in America. Nevertheless, his only real act of philanthropy was witnessed at his deathbed when he donated $400,000 to build the New York Public Library. The rest of his estate was left to his son, William Backhouse.

Capitalism flourished on America's soil, and our limited democratic government did not hinder the pursuit of material wealth. French political thinker Alexis de Tocqueville observed in the late 1830s that "Americans' chief business is to secure for themselves a government which allows them to acquire the things they covet, and which will not debar them from the peaceful enjoyment of those possessions which they have already acquired."

The Civil War made America the second most powerful securities market on the planet. Once again, the government was in need of funds to finance its war efforts. Some of the capital needed was raised when the government instituted income taxes and created the Internal Revenue Service. However, the vast majority of funds came from selling bonds on Wall Street. Investors snapped them up once they realized that much of the money the government was spending was profiting companies like railroads and iron mills.

Wall Street grew dramatically as railroad expansion was financed through securities, and the telegraph—the Victorian

"Internet"—made for instant communication. In 1878, the New York Stock Exchange (NYSE) consisted of only fifty-four companies—thirty-six railroad, five coal, four telegraph, four express, three mining, one steamship, and one land. When the Dow Industrials were first published in 1896, it consisted of just twelve stocks and closed their first day of trading at 40.94. Today, General Electric is the only company that remains from the original Dow list.

Railroads were the blue-chip stocks of the day, not the Industrials—they were considered somewhat like today's better recognized Internet stocks. Sound farfetched? Consider that for 2,000 years, from Alexander the Great to George Washington, people, animals, wind, or water powered man's potential. These four things controlled the world's greatest men of wealth and power.

For example, consider Süleyman the Magnificent, who united the Arab world under the Ottoman empire, and Genghis Kahn, who created the largest land empire ever by conquering half of the known world. Both could travel and conquer only as fast as their feet, horses, or sailboats could carry them.

The Industrial Revolution

The marketplace changed dramatically when James Watt invented the steam engine. It set off the Industrial Revolution in 1760 and caused both technology and industrialization to advance significantly. Yet, the heart of America's capitalistic success was found in its creative capacity and the resourcefulness of its robust individuals. The period between 1890 and 1914 saw the invention of the telephone, camera, phonograph, automobile, airplane, and the electric light bulb—to name but a few.

The Protestant Work Ethic, a limited government that supported capitalism, and technological advancements all combined to increase America's productivity and prosperity. Be that as it may, economic sailing was not always smooth. There were plenty of rough seas along the way. Booms and busts were commonplace in America's emerging capital markets, but people received little or no governmental assistance. They learned to draw strength from their faith and inner reserves.

For example, in the still predominately agrarian economy of 1894, a severe drought devastated farmers, resulting in one-fifth of the workforce being unemployed. Our government, nevertheless, was not willing to provide relief. As then President Grover Cleveland said, "Though the people support the government, the government should not support the people."

During this time, Americans were generally hardworking, resourceful, and rugged. Big business flourished. The new men of wealth became known as industrialists, and real power resided in the hands of only a few, like J.P. Morgan.

J.P. Morgan—*The Most Powerful Man on Wall Street*

Benjamin Franklin discovered electricity, and Thomas Edison harnessed its illuminating power. But it was J.P. Morgan who capitalized on its monetary value by bringing it to Wall Street as the great industrial, General Electric. Morgan, who grew up idolizing Napoleon, found that power became his mistress too.

He became the most powerful man on Wall Street and greatly influenced America's railroad and steel industries. In fact, Morgan became so powerful and influential that he was able to save America twice from impending financial disaster by acting as the de-facto Federal Reserve.

Yet Morgan had become so powerful that Congress determined that too much of the country's financial well-being was concentrated in the hands of one man. Therefore, the Federal Reserve was established, and the Sherman Anti-trust Act was enacted to break up Morgan's behemoth trusts.

When he died, Morgan's estate (excluding his valuable art collection) was worth about $60 million, but none of it was left to charity. Upon learning the value of Morgan's estate, John D. Rockefeller smugly remarked, "Why, that was not enough to make him a rich man!"

The Gospel of Wealth and a Pope's Warning

The sacredness of private property, commercial competition, and accumulation of wealth became the divine law of economics and also influenced our spirituality. Psychologist Carl Jung noted that by the beginning of the twentieth century, "The good Christian was now the enterprising businessman, where worldly goods were the special rewards for his Christian behavior."

Yet, not all were pleased with the progress made under the Gospel of Wealth. A new form of property and labor appeared as capital and wages, which showed no concern for sex, age, or family need. In 1891, Pope Leo XIII voiced concern over the condition of workers during the Industrial Revolution. He urged people to come to the aid of the impoverished since, for the most part, they were in a situation of misfortune and undeserved misery.

Pope Leo stated—"Every principle and every religious feeling has disappeared from the public institutions and so, little by little, isolated and defenseless workers have found themselves at the mercy of inhuman masters and victims of the cupidity of unbridled competition. To this must be added the concentration of industry and commerce in the hands of a few, so that it has become the province of a small number of the rich and opulent, who in this way impose an almost servile yoke in the infinite multitude of the proletariat."

While condemning Communism, the Pope, nonetheless, asked governments to intervene and establish a fair distribution of goods, working hours, weekly rest, and a minimum living wage. The Pope's request, however, fell on deaf ears. In another part of the world around the same time, Communist Karl Marx challenged workers everywhere to unite.

Industrialization and Henry Ford's Model T

Industrialization began to fuel our economy, and Americans were convinced it would ensure that good times were here to stay. We became a nation entrenched in technology, and we could mass-produce like no other. The greatest example of our technological savvy and ability to mass-produce was Henry Ford's Model T.

Ford came up with the idea of the moving assembly line, and his workers became so skilled at using it, they could produce a Model T in 93 minutes. This efficiency enabled Ford to drastically lower prices, while the greater volume made up for lower profit margins. He became so successful at mass-producing cars that he sold over 15 million Model Ts and, for a while, held 50 percent of the automotive market.

But life on Ford's assembly line was harsh. He found it necessary to hire 1,000 men just to keep 100 on the payroll. He ran his assembly lines through fear and intimidation, and many workers felt that they had to give up their dignity to work on them.

When unions came into being, as workers united to challenge the power held by big business, they quickly made their way to Ford's factories. Ford fought against them vehemently. His wife, however, threatened to leave him unless he recognized the unions. Ford begrudgingly gave in, but he was never the same afterward. When he died, he left the bulk of his $1 billion estate to the Ford Foundation. Today, it has assets of nearly $10 billion, making it one of the three largest private foundations in the world.

Unlike that of European nations during World War I, America's industrialization remained largely undeterred. America became the financial safe haven of the world. There was no fighting on our soil, and manufacturing companies received enormous contracts during the war.

For example, Bethlehem Steel received contracts of over ten times the amount they were used to. And how about the Dupont Corporation? It alone provided our allies with 40 percent of their munitions—making the Duponts America's wealthiest family. While other country's economies were in shambles after the war, America emerged as the financial superstar of the world. President Calvin Coolidge summed up the spirit of those times best when he announced to the American people that "the business of America is business!"

Wall Street and Main Street Move in Opposite Directions

In 1925, the top income tax rate was lowered to 25 percent, and billions of dollars were invested in Wall Street as people began speculating on rising stocks. With greed at the helm, the speculative buying craze gained momentum. Many investors began to buy on margin or invested their life savings. They did not realize that insiders were using their positions to skim millions of dollars off the market. The little known reality was, however, that Wall Street and Main Street were moving in opposite directions.

Gross National Product rose less than 50 percent during the 1920s while the Dow quadrupled. Between May 1928 and September 1929, the average stock price rose nearly 50 percent, despite what was going on in the rest of the economy. There were many bank failures, and important sectors like farming and construction were already depressed. The stock market, however, continued to fly first class on an airplane where there was plenty of booze but not enough fuel.

Some on Wall Street were starting to become very uneasy about the market's meteoric rise. Charles Merrill, of today's Merrill Lynch & Co., believed that the financial skies were not clear. The resistance by investors to turning a very substantial profit into cash was an absolute mystery to him. So troubled was Merrill that he went to see a psychiatrist, stating, "Do you think I'm crazy…because I am beginning to think that I must be." The psychiatrist responded, "If you're crazy, then I must be too," and both began selling their holdings before the market crashed.

On September 3, 1929, the Dow Jones industrial average reached an all time high of 381.17. Unfathomable to the unsuspecting public was the market's impending doom. By Thursday, October 24, 1929, Wall Street's airplane finally ran out of fuel. And on Black Tuesday, October 29th, the market crashed. Yet, *The New York Times* that Tuesday morning wrote, "The investor who purchases securities at this time with the discrimination that as always is a condition of prudent investing may do so with utmost confidence." But the *Times* was wrong, as pundits and commentators oftentimes are.

Thousands of investors, many of them ordinary working people, were financially ruined and would never recover. Some could not cope with their financial loss and took a one-way trip through an open window in a downtown office building. But it wasn't just the individual that had fallen from grace. Many banks and businesses that had speculated with their customer's deposits and earnings were also wiped out, furthering a run on the banking system.

As a result of the unbridled consumerism of the 1920s, many newly built mass production facilities turned out goods to the point of over capacity and diminishing marginal returns. It may have seemed like a "field of dreams" in many ways, but simply because production facilities had been built, did not mean that buyers would continue to come. By the time the stock market crashed in 1929, there was a major glut of goods on the market, with factory inventories at three times their normal size.

Another Pope Warns as Calvin's Dreams Fade

In 1929, the richest one percent owned 40 percent of America's wealth. However, the growing number of our nation's poor began to hoard what little money they had. Another Pope, Pius XI, again admonished the rich. He believed that mankind was succumbing to human passions as economics began to divorce itself from moral law and religious virtues.

Pope Pius XI stated, "There has been not merely an accumulation of wealth, but a huge concentration of power and economic dictatorship in the hands of a few who for the most part are not the owners, but merely the trustees and administrators of invested property, handling such funds at their arbitrary pleasure.... This irresponsible power is the natural fruit of unlimited free competition which leaves surviving only the most powerful, which often means the most violent and unscrupulous fighters."

Just how much our human passions were to blame for America's economic plight is debatable, but there was no question that America had entered the Great Depression. The ease with which people spent money and amassed debt was quickly replaced by a hoarding mentality that comes when a nation is gripped by the fear of not being able to afford the basic necessities of life.

It was just a little over 400 years earlier that Calvin envisioned a devout society based on delayed gratification and production, solely for the glory of God. Instead, Americans had indulged themselves with instant gratification and conspicuous consumption. Long gone were the simple days of working solely to provide for one's basic needs.

Consumerism had resulted in the instantaneous fulfillment of many of our temporal wants to the detriment of future economic needs. For many, the price paid for capitalism in the pursuit of a largely materialistic American Dream was much greater than anybody, including Calvin himself, could have foreseen. It was during this economic calamity that most of today's Retirees were reared. Their generation experienced what our ancestors had always known—life is challenging.

"**R**etirees were reared in a time when people weren't as concerned about obtaining affluence as they were with securing peace and the basic necessities of life. Their generation became the steel that was forged through the fires of difficult times."

—Charlie Douglas

Chapter 9

Retirees Embrace Institutions

"Many of today's Retirees were raised
with selfless values, diminished expectations, and a
strong work ethic that stressed teamwork."
—Charlie Douglas—

A few years ago, news anchor Tom Brokaw wrote *The Greatest Generation,* a book about today's Retirees. For the most part, they were born prior to 1946, and today number about 60 million. As the book pointed out, that generation was largely responsible for ensuring many of the freedoms and comforts that we enjoy today. Their generation survived and overcame the challenges of the Great Depression and World War II. As such, many of today's Retirees were raised with selfless values, diminished expectations, and a strong work ethic that stressed teamwork.

Perhaps more than any other characteristic that helped define their generation was that Retirees exhibited enormous faith in our conventional institutions. Many still yearn for the time when our faith will be renewed in these vital institutions. Regarding the events of September 11th, Philip Meyer, consultant to *USA Today,* conveyed the sentiments of many of today's Retirees when he wrote, "Maybe the analogies to Pearl Harbor are overblown. Or maybe not. Please allow me as one of the 12 percent of Americans old enough to remember December 7, 1941, to suggest what it could mean. The good news is that we would start trusting the government again!"

Retirees were reared in a time when people didn't plan to retire early and play golf, or even feel the burden to provide college educations for their children. They weren't as concerned about obtaining affluence as they were with securing peace and the basic necessities of life. Their generation became the steel that was forged through the fires of difficult times.

Hoover and the Fed Underestimate the Economic Downturn

At the beginning of the Depression, President Hoover believed that Americans just needed to bear down a little more and tough it out. Adversity, after all, was part of the price to be paid for free markets to exist under capitalism.

Hoover preached that, in time, the market forces of supply and demand would restore order to the system. Under a protectionistic policy, he raised tariffs on imported goods to keep American workers employed. This backfired, however, as foreign nations imposed higher tariffs, as well, and world trade collapsed. Moreover, the Federal Reserve, which had been battling inflation in a skyrocketing stock market, kept interest rates too high, too long. It failed to provide liquidity, in a timely manner, to an anemic economy.

Hoover had confidence that the American people and capitalism would be resilient. As an accommodation, he cut income taxes, but this offered little relief. Since the average income was only $750 a year, it amounted to only a $4 tax savings. Most people didn't even earn enough to reach the level where they would have to pay income taxes.

In 1932, one-fourth of America was out of work, economic output had declined by 25 percent, and wholesale prices dropped nearly 40 percent. Charles M. Schwab, the head of Bethlehem Steel, said of the Depression, "I'm afraid, every man is afraid." Americans were not unaccustomed to dealing with tough times, but previous periods of adversity seemed, at least, to have an end in sight. During the Great Depression, though, there was little light at the end of the tunnel.

Hoover's Out and Roosevelt's New Deal Is In

Hoover soon discovered that the American people were not as patient as he thought. Their prolonged economic anguish resulted in the election of Franklin Delano Roosevelt, as millions of

Americans found hope with his New Deal and its many relief programs. Roosevelt's government assistance programs, however, caused sizable deficits—the first time this had ever occurred during peacetime.

In his 1935 State of the Union address, Roosevelt acknowledged traditional American policy regarding governmental assistance when he said, "The lessons of history, confirmed by evidence immediately before me, show conclusively that continued dependence upon relief induces a spiritual and moral disintegration fundamentally destructive to the national fiber. To dole out relief in this way is to administer a narcotic, a subtle destroyer of the human spirit. It is in violation of the traditions of America." Nevertheless, like a doctor who prescribes morphine to stop pain, Roosevelt soon found it necessary to increase government programs and budget deficits to finance them.

When faced with difficult times before, Americans had always looked to themselves, their extended families, or perhaps their neighbors to help them meet their immediate needs. The people of this era were not comfortable looking to their government for economic handouts.

In response to the first question ever asked by the Gallup Poll in 1935, "Is the government spending too much money for relief?", 60 percent of the respondents said yes, while fewer than 10 percent thought it was spending too little.

Roosevelt's New Deal, alone, did not end the anguish caused by the Great Depression. Many Americans routinely experienced the degradation of bread lines and soup kitchens. The foolish pride felt by many in the 1920s had turned into despair. The prosperity and promise found in F. Scott Fitzgerald's *The Great Gatsby,* written just a few year's earlier, had been engulfed by the bleakness of John Steinbeck's *The Grapes of Wrath.*

Those who had taken for granted the favorable economic conditions experienced in earlier times were left devastated. Among them were a group of America's greatest businessmen and wealthiest individuals who attended a business meeting in 1923. They included Charles Schwab, head of the largest independent steel company, Bethlehem Steel; Samuel Insull, co-founder of the world's largest utility conglomerate, General Electric; Howard Hopson, head of the largest gas company, Associated Gas & Electric Company; Ivar Krueger, president of one of the world's largest companies at the time, the International Match Co.; Leon Frazier, president of the Bank of International Settlements; Richard Whitney, president of the New York Stock Exchange; Arthur Cotton and Jesse Livermore, two of the biggest speculators on Wall Street; and Albert Fall, a member of President Harding's Cabinet.

Twenty-five years later, history books would recall their lives as follows: Schwab died penniless after living for five years on borrowed money. Insull died broke living in a foreign land. Krueger and Cotton also died broke. Hopson went insane. Whitney and Fall were imprisoned. Fraser and Livermore committed suicide. These men, like many others at the time, had put too much trust in a materialistic world that did not last.

Many people sought to escape the problems of the day, but there was little money for entertainment. Movies became popular, with 60 million Americans each attending a movie every week. Captivating features like *King Kong, Snow White and the Seven Dwarfs,* and *The Wizard of Oz* cost only 15 cents a show.

Those were also the days of the golden age of radio. Many people had their radios turned on all day to keep in touch with the outside world. Shows like *Amos 'n' Andy, Fibber McGee and Molly,* and *The Lone Ranger* filled the air waves as families huddled together in attentive silence. President Roosevelt used this medium skillfully as he administered hope during his fireside chats—to a willing audience that eagerly soaked up his unfailing confidence.

Roosevelt's New Deal had given people hope and prevented the Depression from becoming more severe. In 1937, however, the economy again slipped into recession. The massive government programs created under the New Deal somehow lacked the economic strength needed to pry Americans free from the grip of the Depression. By 1939, the economy was still adrift and the unemployment rate was a staggering 17 percent.

In 1940, daily business and home life was very different from today. More than 20 percent of Americans lived on farms and the majority of the workforce was still blue collar. Few workers had employer-paid health insurance or employer-financed pension plans. There were fewer than one-and-a-half million college students, and only about one in twenty citizens had a college degree.

The majority of Americans were renters, and more than half of all households didn't have a refrigerator. Coal for stoves and furnaces was the main fuel, while most houses didn't have central heating or air conditioning. About one-third of all households didn't even have running water!

Most Retirees grew up without televisions, and only a few households had a telephone or labor-saving devices like an automatic washer or dryer. Women often spent many hours every week dusting floors, furniture, and sills, and washing clothes by hand. Travel was also very limited because commercial jets and interstate highways had yet to be developed.

The Depression Ends as America Enters WWII

The Great Depression finally ended when America entered World War II. Only after the United States had borrowed and spent an additional $1 billion to build its armed forces did America's manufacturing base recover. Few questioned why America was fighting Germany and Japan, and Americans responded readily to Uncle Sam's call, "I Want You!"

Once the war effort was in full swing, unemployment shrank below 2 percent. Although few Americans were buying new appliances, cars, or houses, they were back at work. Most people had ration books and received only a limited supply of gasoline, meat, tires, sugar, and coffee. Americans had become accustomed to doing without. And 64 percent of the respondents said no when a Gallup Poll taken at the beginning of 1945 asked, "Have you had to make any real sacrifices for the war?"

As World War II ended, deficit spending ballooned, resulting in a national debt that was 114 percent the size of the Gross Domestic Product. Taxes tripled, and the top tax rate of 91 percent didn't drop below 88 percent until 1963, when it was lowered to 70 percent.

Wall Street, during this time, went into a long hibernation. Although per capita disposable income was rising dramatically during the early 1940s, investors stayed away from Wall Street. They feared America could still lose the war, and many had been burned during the speculative days leading up to the Great Depression.

The excesses and corruption that led to the market's dramatic rise resulted in the enactment of major reforms. The Securities and Exchange Commission (SEC) was created and headed up by Joseph P. Kennedy, Sr., the father of President John F. Kennedy. Joseph Kennedy was a Wall Street veteran, and it was said that had the SEC existed just 10 years earlier, he would never have become a millionaire. Additionally, the Glass-Steagall Act separated banks from the securities business, and made short selling by corporate officers illegal.

Instead of investing in the market, Americans saved an astounding one-third of what they made. Most put this money into safe, insured savings accounts and war bonds. They also paid down a lot of their consumer debt. The only bright spot for the markets came with the introduction of pension funds. They were designed to supplement Social Security and were demanded by the unions.

Institutional Trust and Mutual Interdependence

During the Great Depression and World War II, Americans became acutely aware of their own humanity and the hardships life can bring. The daily struggles for survival in a severely depressed economy and the horrific destruction of war have a way of bringing people to their knees. For awhile, we looked away from consumption as the source of our happiness and collectively turned to God and each other for support.

Mutual interdependence for day-to-day sustenance and fighting for world peace made those who lived during those days acutely aware of their need for one another. They exhibited tremendous faith in institutions during those trying times and willingly trusted their motives. Institutions like government, family, and religion were all very strong.

These institutions fostered virtues and instilled patriotic values for many who lived through those trying times. America became a community bonded together by a common cause where team-work, and not the fulfillment of the individual, was essential.

Extended families often lived in the same community and sometimes under the same roof. Close relationships were formed during those hard times, and people willingly shared what little they had among family and friends. Married couples seldom di-vorced, not only because of their deep religious faith, but also because it was not an economic option.

Grandchildren forged close relationships with their grandpar-ents, who passed on wisdom cultivated during a lifetime of overcoming difficulties. It wasn't unusual to learn the craft of your father or grandfather. Families also spent a lot of time to-gether. In many cases, Sundays found families together in crowded churches and then off to visit their grandparents for the afternoon. And when someone became ill, the family usually as-sumed the role of primary caregiver, as the words "nursing home" had little relevance.

Americans at that time lost something too. They were no longer masters of their economic domains. It was not the indi-vidual but massive government programs, deficit spending, and the war itself that finally freed many from economic bondage. For many, it was the first time in their lives that individual will and inner reserve, alone, had not been enough to enable them to recover financially. Unaware of the future consequences, Americans began to suckle from the government's bosom, em-powering it to expand its role. Entitlement programs had entered the picture in 1935, when Congress passed the Social Security Act.

For the moment, however, the problems future generations would face were many years away. The bleakness and desola-tion of the previous two decades had become a mere shadow of the past. America was at peace and economically sound. By the end of 1945, Americans had every reason to celebrate and began making babies.

"**D**uring the Baby Boom, America seemed to have everything going for it. With most of our material needs satisfied, there were greater opportunities to begin focusing on personal ideals. Many Boomers were raised to be idealistic, but unfortunately, America's institutions were not ideal."

—Charlie Douglas

Chapter 10

Baby Boomers Question Authority

"Sometime during the Baby Boom, we lost sight of the moral underpinnings of our institutions and our nation. In the process of demythologizing our institutions, we also destabilized many of them."
—Charlie Douglas—

If you grew up a Baby Boomer, you will probably recall your youth with fond memories. At the beginning of the era, big cities such as New York were still clean and safe. Most people left their doors unlocked 24 hours a day. Parents didn't fear that their children's pictures might end up on milk cartons if they walked home late at night.

It was a period when most Americans raised their families in modest homes in the suburbs and pursued stable careers. Our institutions began this time with a renewed strength gained through the hardships of the previous 16 years.

Baby Boomers are those who were born in the United States between 1946 and 1964. Today, there are about 75 million Boomers, representing approximately 28 percent of the U.S. population. They are a major force in our society, as they determine a little over half of the nation's total consumer spending.

Unlike most Retirees, Boomers grew up in relative peace and prosperity, with heightened expectations of individual happiness in a world of renewed consumerism. In time, many Boomers decidedly distanced themselves from conventional institutions.

Boomers Experience a Booming Economy

During the Baby Boom, the pent-up demand created by World War II turned into a dramatic buying binge—the biggest since the

1920s. By 1954, the United States represented less than 10 percent of the world's population, yet produced nearly half of the world's goods. Americans, alone, had nearly 60 percent of the world's cars and telephones, and 45 percent of all radios.

Although the financial underpinnings necessary to lead the stock market higher had been in place for some time, Americans still lacked confidence in the market. Nonetheless, Charles Merrill saw a vast marketing opportunity. The dramatic increase in personal savings rates that occurred during World War II now enabled the public to spend discretionary money. Merrill ingeniously capitalized on the opportunity by bringing Wall Street to Main Street.

Merrill Lynch became the first brokerage house to advertise to the masses, and its employees gave thousands of public seminars throughout America. Investors, once again, became inspired with confidence that Wall Street was a good place to put their money. This helped a new bull market in 1954 break through the old Dow record of 381.17 set in 1929.

Construction and manufacturing were also experiencing bull markets of their own. Before World War II, the average contractor was building five to six houses a year, and most U.S. families did not even own a home. But during the Baby Boom, a man named Bill Levitt shortsightedly believed that, for many, he could simply mass produce the American Dream. As a result of Levitt's vision, his companies built thirty houses a day in a Cape Cod style for a unit cost of about $7,000. By 1955, three out of every four new homes were built in Levitt fashion. Buyers didn't care if their home looked just like their neighbors', so long as they owned a new home.

During the Baby Boom, the gap between the rich and the poor narrowed substantially and, seemingly overnight, many families were financially lifted to a new majority called the "middle class." The world also became a much smaller place as jet airplanes made travel to distant locations a more common reality. Automobiles, too, reached their critical mass among consumers, who used them to travel over thousands of miles of new highways linking major cities.

Three-quarters of the way through the Baby Boom, early Boomers started becoming teenagers, and their spending power began flexing its muscle. They earned about ten dollars a week, a tidy sum in those days. With money to spend, Coonskin Caps, Hula-Hoops®, and a doll named Barbie® were introduced to 20 million Boomers in the 1950s.

The workplace also began to change as the percentage of white-collar employees surpassed blue-collar workers, and the business market started to move away from predominately manufacturing to a more service-oriented economy. For most of America's history, however, goods were purchased sparingly for one's needs and paid for with cash. Now, people bought what they desired and paid later with the introduction of credit cards in 1958.

Television Transforms Our World and Us Along With It

Television was the most transforming development of the Baby Boom era. While fewer than 10 percent of Americans owned one in 1950, 90 percent of all households did by 1962. Television held us spellbound, forever changing the way we experienced the world. Families were captive audiences as the world was brought right into their living rooms. Politics, civil rights, and the cruelty of war in distant lands were all presented in a new light, instantaneously, as things were happening.

By 1954, Americans began moving away from traditional sit-down family dinners at the table, toward eating "TV dinners" in front of the television. FCC (Federal Communications Commission) Chairman Newton Minow declared in 1961 that television, with only three major networks at that time, was a vast wasteland. What would he dare say about television today?

Family life was portrayed by shows such as *Ozzie and Harriett, Father Knows Best, Leave It to Beaver,* and *The Donna Reed Show.* They depicted a nurturing, stay-at-home mother and a well-meaning, career-minded father as the sole provider. Families stayed together and worked through their challenges without the aid of therapy. Life was never portrayed as too exciting, but then Americans had had enough "excitement" during the previous two decades.

Television soon became the world's most effective selling machine, and advertisers shrewdly used it to promote a material-based American Dream. Most advertising targeted women and stressed the point that their role was to keep the family together. Corporations spent lavishly on advertising, hiring experts in psychology to resourcefully appeal to consumers. During this time, Vance Packard wrote the bestseller, *The Hidden Persuaders,* which discussed the various manipulative advertising techniques of the day.

Boomers Are Idealistic but Institutions Are Not Ideal

During the Baby Boom, America seemed to have everything going for it. With most of our material needs satisfied, there were more opportunities for focusing on personal ideals. Pediatrician Dr. Benjamin Spock wrote the world-famous book, *The Common Sense Book of Baby & Child Care,* asserting the need for idealistic children. Accordingly, many Boomers were raised to be idealistic, but, unfortunately, America's institutions were not ideal.

While the Baby Boom continued, there was a growing disparity between what was being beamed into the living room and what was actually going on in real life. Even though today's Retirees were raised with a deep faith in institutions like family, government, business, and religion, Baby Boomers started to question them and, in some cases, rebelled against them.

The girl next door who became the happy homemaker on TV confronted a reality that didn't quite measure up to the fairy tale promised. In the real world, TV's girls next door, like Doris Day, Debbie Reynolds, and Dinah Shore, could not seem to maintain solid family home lives. There were nine divorces among them as they searched for marital bliss.

Technology helped emancipate women during the Baby Boom era, and a growing number of women were no longer content to be housewives. In previous years, women were often physically spent from doing routine housework. Laborsaving appliances, like washers and dryers, once luxuries, became everyday household items during the Baby Boom. And the invention of antibiotics, like penicillin, drastically reduced the time mothers had to spend tending to their children's illnesses.

Like June Cleaver of *Leave It to Beaver,* intelligent women, dressed in pearls and high heels, waited for the daily return of their "all-powerful" husbands. But the scenario wasn't exactly fulfilling itself in real life. Many women began working in earnest outside the household. *The Feminine Mystique* by Betty Friedan helped send a message to women that they could do unconventional things in a man's world, and it quickly became a must read for those participating in the growing feminist movement.

Meanwhile, career-minded fathers were having problems securing ideal jobs in the real world. Many men latched onto the security of big corporations after experiencing the economic instability of the Depression and the daily quest for survival during World War II. As was depicted in the 1955 movie, *The Man in the Gray Flannel Suit,* men with family responsibilities were not willing to risk their economic stability by exploring more fulfilling career options.

Americans also soon discovered that what was good for big corporations, like General Motors, wasn't necessarily good for them too. Companies like GM, at times, placed profits ahead of consumers' best interests by turning out unsafe products like the Corvair automobile.

Even the media that had captivated America's attention began to violate our trust. Television networks were busted for "fixing" game shows like *Twenty-One.* The networks, along with their corporate sponsors who promoted a cheerful lifestyle that belonged only to suburban white families, were now being challenged by civil rights activists like Dr. Martin Luther King.

The most important institution to come under attack, however, was the family. The idealized image of the happy family, which had been skillfully spun together, started to come apart at the seams. In the real world, family life was often strained as people were marrying far too young—at an average age of 18 in 1955—to know who they were and what they wanted.

What was supposed to have been blissful family life in communities all over America was, at times, scandalous and not unlike those indiscretions portrayed in Grace Metalious's *Peyton Place.* In the real world, families fought and couples were not always faithful. After conducting the most expansive sexual survey ever, Alfred Kinsey stunned Americans by claiming that 50 percent of married men and 25 percent of married women had been unfaithful.

Boomers Encounter the Sexual Revolution

Hugh Hefner started publishing *PlayBoy* in 1953. The magazine was promoted as one of style and charm that often appealed to educated readers. His first nude centerfold, Marilyn Monroe, became known as a sex symbol, the most popular the world has ever known.

Some Boomers who were old enough took part in America's sexual revolution. A less-reproachful term, "premarital sex," quickly replaced its religious counterpart, fornication. And the advent of rock and roll, with Elvis Presley leading the way, helped rouse the emotions of young adults and forever changed the course of music.

Aided by the invention of the birth control pill in 1960, Boomers were the first generation of young adults to experience "free love." Although the pill was designed to prevent unwanted pregnancies for married couples, unmarried woman could also have sex without the fear of pregnancy.

More Guns and Butter at the Same Time

At the start of the Baby Boom, America's government was committed to a balanced budget. That's not to say that balanced budgets always existed. In fact, budget deficits often occurred for brief periods during times of war and, to a lesser extent, during severe economic times such as the Depression.

Under President Truman, America balanced four of seven budgets from 1946 to 1952. President Eisenhower also saw a balanced budget as a necessary discipline. Eisenhower's message was simple: "…in good times at the very least, we should pay our own way, and we should not have more government than the people are willing to pay for with taxes." In 1954, defense spending still accounted for 70 percent of the federal budget, and Eisenhower warned that America could not have more guns and more butter at the same time.

In 1961, President Kennedy uttered his immortal inaugural words, "Ask not what your country can do for you. Ask what you can do for your country," challenging all Americans to do something for America. Nonetheless, Kennedy's administration helped provide Americans with ever-increasing public services.

People started to depend more on corporate pension plans and Social Security than on their individual savings. Likewise, healthcare shifted from individual responsibility to institutional responsibility. The majority of it was either paid for by the employer or funded through government insurance.

President Kennedy and his administration similarly introduced a new view of economics and budget deficits too. Whereas deficit spending had been used only to prime the pump in times of war or severe economic hardship, it began being used to monitor the economy and minimize sluggish periods during normal business cycles. No longer did deficits carry the moral stigma they once did. They were now considered legitimate means to accomplish a worthwhile political end.

During President Johnson's term in office, his administration helped push the deficit ceiling higher by establishing more programs than our government could financially support. In 1964, President Johnson declared war on poverty, and America's "Great Society" came into full existence with the introduction of Medicare.

It was honorable to want to eradicate injustices by trying to improve the quality of life for so many through the use of government. That was a noble pursuit. The trouble, however, was that the United States government was now taking on a much larger role than Americans were willing to support or, for that matter, than our Founding Fathers had ever intended.

The Fear of Communism Abounds

While Boomers questioned nearly all institutions, they openly challenged their government the most. And no issue was more troubling to Boomers than our government's use of military force to stop the spread of Communism.

During the Baby Boom generation, the fear of Communism abounded. We fought both the Korean War and the Cold War to deter the spread of Communism. In fact, the fear of Communism was so entrenched that Senator Joseph McCarthy exploited it by accusing hundreds of State Department employees of being Communist Party members.

The Vietnam War began as a war of containment against Communism. However, two days after President Kennedy's shocking assassination by an alleged Communist sympathizer, Lee Harvey Oswald, President Johnson stated, "It is the United States' goal to help the Saigon government to military victory."

As the war escalated, President Johnson believed, in good faith, that by applying greater amounts of pressure against the North Vietnamese, he could bring them to the negotiating table and achieve victory. Unfortunately, President Johnson misjudged the mindset of those people who said, through their leader Ho Chi Min, "For every ten of us you kill, we kill one of you, and in the end we will win."

Before the Vietnam War ended, many Baby Boomers would do more than question their government and the establishment—they would protest against them. A chorus of Boomer voices began chanting, "Hell no, we won't go!" and "Hey, hey, LBJ, how many more did you kill today?"

The oldest and more outspoken Boomers protested on college campuses and burned draft cards. Some left America altogether for safer pastures in Canada. Still others let their hair grow long, took drugs, participated in love-ins, and were branded by the establishment as hippies.

The establishment fought back by jailing those who burned draft cards. It used military force at times to quash anti-war rallies. At Kent State University, four students would die at the hands of National Guardsmen at a demonstration that got out of hand. Even the "greatest of all time," the newly ordained Muslim, Mohammed Ali, was stripped of his World Boxing title when he refused to enter the military.

The Generation That Forgot God

America's religious institutions were not spared from criticism either. Boomers argued that religion had become irrelevant and too distant. The "we" of community that had served Retirees well while growing up was starting to give way to the "I" of personal devotion. Toward the end of the Baby Boom generation, many people stopped turning to organized religion for meaning.

Religious institutions found it necessary to change their interpretation and the expression of their message in order to adapt to a changing world. For example, Vatican II, the Second Vatican Council, was held during the early 1960s in an effort to modernize the message of the Catholic Church—so it could meet the challenges of contemporary times.

Yet, despite the positive changes that came out of Vatican II, there was a decline in Church attendance and baptisms, and fewer men were seeking to become priests. A reduced number of marriages were being performed in the Church, as the practice of "living together" (out of wedlock) rose dramatically. Other denominations were also experiencing declines of participation in religious practices.

It was not only priests, rabbis, and pastors who suffered. Many other figures of authority—teachers, police, and politicians—were now questioned by Boomers. But even so, much of the falling away from God and organized religion that occurred at the end of the Baby Boom period still remains somewhat of a mystery.

Perhaps Beatle John Lennon offered the best explanation when, in 1966, he said, "Most young people are more interested in rock-'n'-roll than in religion.... The Beatles are more popular than Jesus now." *Time* magazine captured the sentiment of the day in April 1966 by printing an issue titled "IS GOD DEAD?" Twenty-seven years later, an April 1993 cover of *Time* labeled Boomers "THE GENERATION THAT FORGOT GOD."

As the Baby Boom era came to an end, America had decisively moved away from traditional values, religious virtues, and the institutions that promoted them. During the mid-'60s, Harvey Cox Jr., Harvard theologian, made clear in his bestselling book, *The Secular City*, that mainstream institutions and religious beliefs were on the decline. Government, corporate, familial, and religious institutions were all considerably weakened, and we no longer placed blind trust in them.

The spiritual capital and patriotism produced in earlier times were on the wane. Sometime during the Baby Boom, we lost sight of the moral underpinnings of our institutions and our nation. In the process of demythologizing our institutions, we also destabilized many of them. Into this unstable environment a new generation was born—Generation X.

"No generation since the Depression has been set up for failure like this. Everything the dot-com boom delivered has been taken away and then some."

—*Forbes* Magazine, 2002

Chapter 11

Generation X Gets No Respect

*"Traditional values
that our institutions helped impart to earlier
generations had little opportunity to take root in Xers."*
—Charlie Douglas—

Generation X, like Rodney Dangerfield, got no respect. There are approximately 75 million people who belong to this generation that were born between 1965 and 1976. The family units in which many Xers were raised found more parents divorcing and fetuses being aborted.

Economically, Xers witnessed the recessionary impact of double-digit inflation, a drastic stock market decline, the worst savings and loan crisis since the Depression, and a corporate America that was downsizing.

Xers were treated as a low priority when allocating benefits, yet the government demanded they pay a proportionately larger share in taxes. Spiritually, Xers were exposed far less to traditional religious institutions and more often to the unsteadiness of contemporary movements.

The Family Unit Begins to Break Down

While most Boomers as children enjoyed a relatively secure family life, Xers experienced the instability that comes when family units begin to break down. During Generation X, birthrates dropped dramatically, and would-be mothers throughout the 1970s aborted one fetus out of every three pregnancies.

Many parents decisively moved away from the long-held traditional belief that they needed to stay together in order to properly raise their children. Xers were three times more likely to experience a parental breakup than were Boomers. Unfortunately for Xers, America's divorce rate doubled during their generation.

Demand for day-care facilities also increased with Generation X. Unlike Boomers, Xers saw millions of their mothers flock into the work force as the proportion of preschoolers cared for by stay-at-home moms fell roughly by one-half.

With working mothers becoming more commonplace, many Xers reported that they shouldered considerable responsibility in raising themselves. As a generation, many Xers found solace through television in an otherwise empty home. The typical 14-year-old watched three hours of television a day and did only one hour of homework.

Television shows like *The Courtship of Eddie's Father, The Brady Bunch,* and *The Partridge Family* made it clear that the nuclear family of the '50s and '60s had changed. Now children were merging together in the blended families of multiple marriages or living in single-parent households.

Corporate Downsizing, Inflation, and a Bear Market

Many Xers witnessed their parents looking for work because of a new process known as corporate downsizing. After World War II, big corporations implicitly promised their employees guaranteed paychecks and attractive benefits. But the favorable economic climate enjoyed during most of the Baby Boom changed. During Generation X, a plethora of corporations failed to make good on implied promises.

Big companies once took great pride in being able to make statements like IBM did in their company handbook, titled *About Your Company*, prepared in 1981—"In nearly 40 years, no person employed on a regular basis by IBM has lost as much as one hour of working time because of a layoff. When recessions come or there is a major product shift, some companies handle the work-force imbalances by letting people go. IBM hasn't done that and hopes it never has to do so. People are a treasured resource. It's hardly a surprise that one of the main reasons people like to work for IBM is the company's all-out effort to maintain full employment."

But many IBM employees were sorely surprised between 1986 and 1994, when the company cut its work force essentially in half. IBM was not alone as a host of other bellwether names, including the likes of General Motors, AT&T, Sears, Ford, Xerox, and Citicorp also implemented significant layoffs.

Downsizing became necessary because of the harsh economic conditions caused by the recessions of the 1970s and early 1980s. And a loose credit system, deficit spending for bigger government, the Vietnam War, and higher oil prices all combined to produce runaway inflation that climbed to an all-time high of 13½ percent in 1980.

Inflation, too, became a formidable adversary for Generation X. President Nixon spent most of his presidency fighting the inflation caused by the guns-and-butter of the Vietnam War and the Great Society. Inflation continued to soar during the Carter Administration to levels not seen since the Civil War. When Ronald Reagan came into office, he and Federal Reserve Board Chairman Paul Volker took drastic measures to fight inflation as the prime rate soared to 20 percent, while unemployment rose to 10 percent.

Inflation also weighed heavily on the stock market as the worst bear market transpired since the Great Depression. The Standard & Poors 500, on an inflation-adjusted basis, lost 50 percent of its value between late 1968 and late 1982. On top of the market's woes was the savings and loan crisis which occurred during the late 1980s and early 1990s. Hundreds of savings and loans needed to be bailed out at a cost of $500 billion.

The Government Offers Little Reassurance for Xers

Our government offered little moral reassurance to Xers, as the most famous modern-day political scandal in American history occurred in 1972. The Watergate break-in and cover-up unraveled a web of political spying, bribery, and the illegal use of campaign funds. The disclosure of these activities resulted in the indictments of some 40 government officials and the resignation of President Nixon. Years later, actress Meg Ryan spoke for many Xers when she said, "I think I have a deep distrust of authority. I'm a Watergate baby."

Xers also experienced a time when our government began investing less of its resources in its future, using them instead for generations born earlier. For example, Social Security and Medicare expenses grew exponentially during Generation X. And while many Retirees will collect Social Security benefits amounting to more than three times what they put in, Xers were told that Social Security would be a mere pittance by the time they retired.

Despite increasing amounts spent on entitlements, the United States has one of the highest rates of childhood poverty among all industrialized nations. Xers are much more likely to be below the poverty line than are Retirees.

Although Xers anticipate receiving far less of the benefits' pie, the government expects them to pay far more in current taxes. For example, in 1990, a Generation X couple with a baby and one parent earning $30,000 a year, paid five times as much in taxes as the typical Retiree with a similar income from public and private pensions.

Deficits also rose dramatically during Generation X as the government spent heavily during the Cold War. As our military was built up to out-muscle the Soviet Union, our national deficit swelled to $4 trillion. Annual interest payments, alone, were $200 billion. Many Xers felt that those in power had the luxury to ignore the swelling debt they were leaving to them.

America's infrastructure also paid a heavy price to win the Cold War. From federal highways to public school systems, many government programs were scaled back. And some segments were more affected by the cutbacks than others. The timing could not have been worse for the U.S. Department of Education. It was already warning that there was a "rising tide of mediocrity" that was surfacing in our nation's schools in its published report titled, "A Nation at Risk."

Xers Are Not Easy to Find on Main Street

It was the individual and one's differences that were highlighted during Generation X, not what was common among us.

Earlier generations experienced advertising and marketing that was intended for the masses, stressing what was collectively shared. During the Xer generation, however, advertisers and marketers continued to segment and subdivide America into smaller market fragments through *target marketing* and *niche advertising*. No wonder nine out of ten Xers agreed that there was a time when people in this country felt they had more in common and shared more values than Americans do today.

Xers didn't have much of a cause to rally around and bring them together. While Retirees and Boomers might look to movies like *Saving Private Ryan* or *Platoon* as defining moments, the short-lived war efforts in Operation Desert Storm weren't sufficient to unite Xers in the same way.

Consider that during every 100 hours on American inner-city streets, three times more of our youth lost their lives in gunfire than were killed in the 100 hours of Operation Desert Storm. And while joining the military may have been a safer alternative than street gangs, nevertheless, it was street gangs that seemed to offer many of America's disconnected youth a real chance to belong.

Unfortunately, most of today's young Americans know less and care less about news and public affairs than do the generations that came before them. Many Xers today feel little connection to the broader issues of the world, and they are less inclined to identify with mainstream America.

As a whole, Xers are less likely to vote as compared with Boomers and Retirees. But when Xers do vote, they frequently do so as Independents, often supporting candidates who, likewise, have disdain for the status quo. For instance, a candidate like ex-pro wrestler Jessie Ventura, Minnesota's former governor, was an overwhelming favorite among Minnesota Xers. During his governorship, many Xers proudly displayed bumper stickers on their cars that read, "My governor can beat up your governor!"

Religious Choices Without a Solid Spiritual Foundation

Traditional religious institutions also had minimal impact in shaping the values of many Xers. Unfortunately, about the time the first Xers were born, Americans were noticeably distancing themselves from their conventional concept of God and religion.

As Xers' parents searched for their own faiths, Xers were exposed more to New Age and Evangelical sects. And while Xers may have valued their freedom to choose, many did not receive a solid spiritual foundation on which to make informed decisions.

In a culture where today's youth increasingly pierce, tattoo, or otherwise disfigure their bodies—once thought to be sacred temples—one might question if some of them have any spiritual convictions at all. Nevertheless, Tom Beaudoin, the author of the book, *Virtual Faith,* notes that "Tattooing and piercing signify a need to be deeply marked." Moreover, he continues, "Young adults satisfy their spiritual hunger by using these piercings and tattoos as their own sacramentals, partly because they see that religious institutions are unable to provide for deeply marking, profoundly experiential encounters."

An article in the *The Wall Street Journal* in the late 1990s reported, "Today's youth seek ancient rituals and mysticism as churches and synagogues compete with Eastern and New Age religion—as well as paganism, gangs, cults, and 12-step programs, which all offer the rituals that appeal to some young people."

Entire teen clothing lines became devoted to dark, mystical-looking "Goth" fashion. Perhaps there was more to worry about than "Medieval" clothing, as the *Journal* also reported of an Episcopal Church in New York that became bored with the same old Christmas pageant complaining that "it was always the one with the Virgin Mary." So, instead, they wrote a new one with characters from the cynical cartoon *South Park* to communicate its message.

Not surprisingly, Generation Xers are the least likely adult generation to have a religious affiliation or regularly attend a traditional place of worship. Professor Jeffrey Arnett of the University of Missouri-Columbia, who has studied Generation X in detail, reports that only 15 to 20 percent attend conventional faith communities with any regularity. Alas, religion ranked behind friends, home, school, music, and TV as factors Xers believed had the greatest influence on their generation, according to the George H. Gallup International Institute.

Is the "Golden Ladder" the Xers' Way Out?

Traditional values that our institutions helped impart to earlier generations had little opportunity to take root in Xers. Our weakened institutions weren't available to them on any meaningful basis. Unable to depend on these institutions for support, many Xers made their own way.

Enabled by the technology of an industry that began in earnest in 1977, when Steven Jobs founded Apple Computer out of a home garage, the personal computer greatly assisted many Xers who decided to bet on themselves. *The Wall Street Journal* once stated of Xers, "This generation is more willing to gamble their careers than earlier generations," as many had started their own small businesses. What a difference a few decades made; 40 years earlier, hardly anybody wished to take on the risk of being self-employed.

But the economic prosperity that occurred for numerous others during the 1980s and 1990s seems like a pipe-dream to many Xers today. In October 2002, *Fortune* magazine had this to say of Xers—"No generation since the Depression has been set up for failure like this. Everything the dot-com boom delivered has been taken away and then some. Real wages are falling, wealth continues to shift from younger to older, and education costs are surging. Worse yet, for some Gen Xers, their peak earning years are behind them. Buried in college and credit card debt, a lot of them won't be able to catch up...."

Xers were born far too late to embrace the words of President Franklin D. Roosevelt: "The very objectives of young people have changed, away from the dream of the golden ladder, [which is] each individual for himself, and toward a broad highway on which thousands of your fellow men and women are advancing."

On the contrary, our institutional base did not provide a promising future for Xers' collective advancement. As other generations advanced their economic positions, scores of Xers came to believe that the golden ladder may be the only thing left of the American Dream that provides a way out.

Consider that, according to *Roper College Track*, "Three quarters of American college seniors during Generation X said that it will be harder for their generation to achieve the American Dream than it was for the last generation." It should also come as little surprise that a 1989 Gallup Poll found that nearly 80 percent of adults thought young people were more selfish and materialistic today than they were 20 years ago.

Before the implosion of the NASDAQ in March of 2000, an online trading commercial captured the sentiment of numerous Xers—"We're not relying on the government; we're not relying on the company; we're not relying on some big fat inheritance; we're relying on ourselves. We plan to retire rich!" Unfortunately, Xers could not even rely on online trading. Comparatively speaking, Rodney Dangerfield seemed to be getting a lot more respect.

"It feels good to hear the President say that the state of our Union has never been stronger, and Lee Greenwood's perform-ance of "God Bless the U.S.A." is inspirational. Nevertheless, the strength of our Union and the foundation of the American Dream rest squarely on values, virtues, and staying connected to our Creator— not just on a pot of gold at the end of the rainbow."

—Charlie Douglas

Chapter 12

The State of Our Union

*"As the American Dream has been passed down from
Retirees to Boomers to Xers, there has been a distancing from our
exposure to traditional religious virtues and patriotic values.
As time has passed, the community reserve of spiritual
capital has noticeably declined."*
—Charlie Douglas—

On Thursday, September 20, 2001, President George W.
Bush spoke from the floor of the House of Representatives and said—"My fellow citizens, for the last nine
days, the entire world has seen for itself the state of our union,
and it is strong!"

Four months later, he spoke to us again delivering the State
of the Union Address. He began with these words—"As we
gather together tonight, our nation is at war, our economy is in
recession, and the civilized world faces unprecedented dangers.
Yet the state of our Union has never been stronger!"

America is strong and the only remaining superpower. Our
military is second to none and is equipped to simultaneously fight
two wars on different parts of the globe. However, many are beginning to question the fidelity of non-economic assets on which
the state of our Union rests. Consider that in the 1950s, about 70
percent of Americans said they trusted the federal government to
do the right thing most of the time. Today, only about 30 percent
express such trust.

A Wavering Public Sector

Over the past few years, all too often polls, not sound principles, have dictated our leaders' actions and our perceptions of them. In our volatile environment, leaders too often yield to current public sentiment in order to protect their positions in office. Our republic, nevertheless, needs to reflect principled leaders of conviction, whom we entrust to make tough decisions that further meaningful societal interests. The Founding Fathers began with a healthy Constitutional distance, that is, safeguards, between electing those who would decide and what was ultimately decided. Imagine what our country might look like today if our nation's greatest leaders, like Washington, Lincoln, and Roosevelt, had made their magnanimous decisions based on opinion polls or some focus group's recommendation.

Character is no longer the primary factor by which we judge those who hold our highest political offices. During the Clinton administration, it became glaringly apparent that we were willing to overlook suspect character in our elected officials as long as the economy was in good shape. Even though you cannot legislate character or integrity, it appears that our leaders are being increasingly elected, judged, and kept in office primarily based on one overwhelming factor: "It's the economy, stupid!"

When we vote in favor of our pocketbooks at the expense of our principles, however, we diminish the spiritual capital that can be utilized today and by future generations. To a large degree, we are still living off the non-economic assets that were entrusted to us with the immortal words inscribed on the Iwo Jima memorial: "When uncommon valor was a common virtue."

Over time, there has been a gradual decay in our commitment to patriotic principles. Many of us have become desensitized to conduct that used to offend our moral heritage. Actions that may have been considered reprehensible in the past may no longer incite us in the present. "Shock-jocks," like Howard Stern, are becoming more accepted by mainstream America, and they keep raising the "provocative conduct bar" to new heights.

But as Pope John Paul II has warned, "If there is no truth to guide and direct political activity, then ideals and convictions can easily be manipulated for reasons of power. History demonstrates, a democracy without values easily turns into open or thinly disguised totalitarianism."

The Private Sector and Our Misplaced Trust

According to a Pew Forum Survey, conducted in March 2002, Americans now think more highly of Washington politicians than they do business executives. And later in 2002, *USA Today* reported, "More than seven in ten Americans say they distrust CEOs of large corporations, as nearly eight in ten believe that top executives of large companies will take improper actions to help themselves at the expense of their companies."

In this post-Enron environment, many have painfully discovered the grim consequences of misplaced trust. The betrayal of investor confidence, which is near an all-time low, is causing many to cling to the sidelines or head for the exit. Consider the following exploitations:

Many Wall Street analysts and investment banks, time and again, gave us tainted research crafted in "workshops full of conflicts of interest." A significant number of analysts who were employed by investment banks irresponsibly placed "strong buy" ratings on many tech and telecom stocks, in particular, to perpetuate the illusion of company and industry-wide growth. For them, it was the accepted way of securing that company's investment banking business. As a result, some research analysts at Merrill Lynch and other brokerage houses publicly pumped up stocks that they privately scorned in order to acquire business.

At times, investment banking firms played both sides of the fence too. In Enron's case, those firms were not only some of the main investment bankers, but also some of the largest investors who profited the most from Enron's questionable partnerships.

Chief Congressional Investigators reported that Enron would not have been able to engage in their accounting deceptions had it not been for the active participation of certain major financial institutions. These collaborative entities went along with and even helped expand Enron's activities. Unprincipled lawyers also aided Enron in gaining access to capital and security markets.

Historical guardians of financial information, like Arthur Anderson, also had a hard time objectively carrying out their audits on the Enrons and WorldComs of the world. The staggering tax consulting fees they were paid were too tempting to pass up. (Anderson's fees to Enron were projected to be up to $100 million for 2001.) In fact, during 2001, tax consulting fees industry-wide brought in three times the amount of revenue as compared to that brought in by auditing fees.

Dishonest CEOs, in a few cases, pillaged the very companies they were entrusted to manage and protect. For example, the founder and former head of Adelphia has been charged with looting the nation's sixth largest cable company to pay for luxury condos, a golf course, and to help cover personal investment losses. Likewise, the former CEO of Tyco International Ltd., Dennis Kozlowski, has been charged with raiding the company of about $600 million.

Home-decorating diva Martha Stewart, a former stockbroker, is another interesting case. She did not plunder Martha Stewart Living Omnimedia's assets directly. Nevertheless, it appears that her attempt to save $46,000 in losses on an "improper stock sale" will, at a minimum, end up costing her, as well as Omnimedia's shareholders, hundreds of millions.

Boardroom conflicts of interest existed among directors and the stockholders they purportedly represented. In theory, boards of directors are supposed to represent stockholders independently. However, that becomes problematic when many directors are handpicked by the respective CEOs. More distressing is the fact that during the summer of 2002, 75 percent of the S&P 500 companies revealed that their CEOs and Chairmen of the Boards were the same people. And for a period of time after the mandate that Wall Street reform itself, Dick Grasso, Chairman of the NYSE, continued to serve as a director for Home Depot. However, he demonstrated exemplary leadership by resigning from Home Depot's board, thereby removing the potential for partiality.

Be that as it may, Warren Buffet wrote in a recent editorial: "To clean up their acts on these fronts, CEOs don't need independent directors, oversight committees, or auditors absolutely free of conflicts and exercising 'good' business ethics. They simply need to do what is right." Buffet's words are easier said than done. As James Madison noted, "If men were angels no government would be necessary."

Doing what is right demonstrates business ethics—which need to be the heart of America's free market system. Laws can only persuade proper conduct; they cannot instill integrity or personal responsibility. It takes business ethics, which are nothing more than personal ethics.

Unfortunately, the reality is that self-regulation in our free market economic system has failed miserably over the last few years. Without state securities regulators like New York's Attorney General, Eliot Spitzer, there most likely would not have been any consequential action at all taken against unprincipled investment banking conduct.

Even with Sptizer's assistance, the Securities and Exchange Commission managed to structure a settlement of only $1.4 billion in the aggregate from 10 of the nation's biggest brokerage firms in question. Although it represented the largest settlement on record, it, nevertheless, was a pittance compared to the huge losses incurred by innocent investors. Furthermore, that modest amount is not likely to serve as a meaningful deterrent against future acts of impropriety.

The 90s were another "boom" period in America's economic history when business ethics, in more than a few cases, were cast aside in the chase for material gain. A self-governing marketplace and a democracy, nevertheless, are only as good as their self-governing individuals. Personal ethics, when divorced from spirituality and religious virtues, more often than not become relative and impotent.

Contrary to Some People's Belief—*Greed Is NOT Good*

As Alan Greenspan said in the Federal Reserve Board's semi-annual monetary policy report to Congress in July of 2002, "Lawyers, internal and external auditors, corporate boards, Wall Street security analysts, rating agencies, and large institutional holders of stock all failed for one reason or another to detect and blow the whistle on those who breached the level of trust essential to well-functioning markets."

But America's businesses are not inherently corrupt. Many honorable and faith-filled citizens are at the helm of these vital institutions. Much of the problem, however, stems from the fact that the majority of businesses are fixated upon the short-term bottom line. Wall Street offers little consolation for those companies who may have taken current charges against profitability in order to build for the longer term. Financial capital and executive compensation are both clearly tied to their immediate bottom lines.

Today, some business executives receive hundreds of millions of dollars in annual compensation based primarily on their companies' current performance—even though that may be in conflict with what's truly best for those companies in the long term. Bonuses, stock options, and promotions are all closely tied to how to make the companies more profitable currently. Since we typically reward those at the helm for performance, some executives self-servingly manipulate the bottom line.

With tremendous pressure to perform and intense global competition, some companies have stopped making prudent longer-term investments in their most precious resource—their people. Today, more and more employees are being let go to cut costs. Perhaps too little attention is being paid to effectively balance today's bottom line with employee contentment and long-term profitability.

Gordon Gekko's viewpoint from the movie, *Wall Street,* that "Greed is good," may have helped propel the market's advance. However, this same mindset awakened a ferocious bear market. Take, for example, Andrew Fastow, former CFO of Enron. He wasn't satisfied just being a millionaire with fine automobiles and an 11,000-square-foot mansion. He also believed that some of the money he siphoned from Enron was owed to him. His greed led him to rationalize that "no one had done more for Enron than Andy Fastow."

Perhaps Federal Reserve Chairman Alan Greenspan expressed it best when he said, "People today aren't greedier than people in the past, it is just that the avenues to express greed are so vast." As with so many things in life, investing is an act of faith requiring trust. Without faith and confidence that a company's financials reflect reality, our capital markets simply cannot function properly.

Increasing shareholder wealth requires the public's trust, which depends upon ethical business practices. If you remove the non-economic asset of integrity from the marketplace, the constructive interplay regarding all other economic assets comes to a grinding halt.

Ethical values ultimately affect all facets of society—not just business practices on Wall Street. Syndicated columnist Chuck Colson put it this way: "Societies are tragically vulnerable when the men and women who compose them lack character. A nation or culture cannot endure for long unless it is under-girded by common values such as valor, public-spiritedness, and respect for others and for the law; it cannot stand unless it is populated by people who will act on motives superior to their own immediate interests."

Families Have Their Own Challenges

Former Senator Patrick Moynihan of New York said the biggest change he had seen in his 40-year political career was that the family structure had come apart all over North America. There is plenty of evidence to back Moynihan's claim. Since 1960, the divorce rate has more than doubled; out-of-wedlock births have gone from one in twenty to one in three, and the percentage of single-parent families has more than tripled. And yet, the most important institution charged with forming moral character is the family. In his book, *The Broken Hearth,* William J. Bennett states, "The family has suffered a blow that has no historical precedent—and one that has enormous ramifications for American society."

The technological advancements of recent years have failed to provide greater opportunities for parents to spend more quality time with their children. More and more working couples and single parents are discovering that nannies and day-care centers are ill-equipped to impart meaningful values to today's youth. "Family values," so casually paraded around during political campaigns are, nonetheless, vital to our nation's well-being and our sense of morality.

Many children and young adults are spending more time watching television, using the Internet, or playing computer-driven games than personally interacting with their peers. In our quest for technological advancement, we may be unknowingly creating an environment where our children are becoming more comfortable with things than they are with one another.

By the time our children become teenagers, on average, they have already spent three years in front of televisions, some of it watching MTV or VH-1, which often border on "soft porn." And a favorite video game among our youth today, which has won numerous "Game of the Year" awards, is a trip to the party capital of America called "Grand Theft Auto Vice City™," where players can interact with hookers, gangsters, and corrupt politicians.

Television, in many cases, only serves to heighten expectations and stimulate our consumer appetites to buy, buy, buy. And as religious historian Robert Bellah commented, "That happiness is to be attained through limitless acquisition is denied by every religion and philosophy known to mankind, but is preached incessantly by every American television set."

In our neighborhoods, we are experiencing far less face-to-face contact than we did 50 years ago, which has led to a decline in our sense of community and need for one another. Weekly trips to Wal-Mart, Home Depot, and Blockbuster aren't exactly community-building events. As corporations increased in size to gain competitive advantage, we started losing touch with the mom and pop shops that helped create a sense of community and common identity.

Religion's Credibility Crisis

In a world already shaken by terrorism and economic insecurity, religious institutions can ill-afford the current controversies. The April 1, 2002 cover of *Time* bluntly asks the question: "CAN THE CATHOLIC CHURCH SAVE ITSELF?" Likewise, the May 6, 2002 cover of *Newsweek* asks another compelling question: "WHAT WOULD JESUS DO?—Christianity at a Crossroads."

We would do well to note that America is quickly becoming the most religiously diverse nation on the planet. Though still overwhelmingly Christian (more than 90 percent), there are now more Buddhists than Presbyterians, and nearly as many Muslims as Jews. In recent times, America has been expanding its Judeo-Christian heritage to include Islamic, Hindu, and Buddhist cultures. By any contemporary measure, America is not an irreligious nation; it is a multi-faith nation.

But one may ask, "Who needs God and religion today? Couldn't rational conduct composed of moral atheists accomplish the same goal?" In theory, yes, because love is the ultimate rational act. The problem with that theory, however, is that throughout the course of humanity, loving, rational conduct has never occurred with any real degree of success for a prolonged period of time apart from God and religious virtues.

Without staying connected to the source of all love and a guiding purpose that is greater than ourselves, our actions are largely self-centered. Throughout history, our reliance upon a loving God never got us into trouble. It was an ego-based dependence on ourselves and our divisiveness toward one another that led us astray.

"Great Necessities Call Out Our Great Virtues"

Today, a diminishing base of spiritual capital adversely affects our institutions as well as each of us. Every generation is impacted. If Retirees are the "greatest generation," it may very well be that the calamitous circumstances they faced demanded greatness from them. As women's rights activist Abigail Adams pointed out, "Great necessities call out our great virtues."

Within each generation, there are those who are largely self-seeking and materialistic, as well as those who are often unselfish and spiritually oriented. Espousing generational superiority and reminiscing about the good old days can present a rather limited view of our world. In the present, there is a tendency toward the belief that we are on some slippery slope, but the past can oftentimes be recast as an ascent toward a noble ambition. Yet, there has never been a time when the Founding Fathers would have found the state of our nation in complete harmony with their original virtuous desires.

Patrick Henry was deeply concerned about the decline of morality after the Revolutionary War. Likewise, Abraham Lincoln warned that the indispensable virtues that the Revolutionary War taught were being leveled by the silent artilleries of time. And the Roaring 20s didn't exactly find America on top of the moral high ground. Nevertheless, religious principles and patriotic values were much more a part of the moral fabric of our society in years past than they are today.

As the American Dream has been passed down from Retirees to Boomers to Xers, there has been a distancing from our exposure to traditional religious virtues and patriotic values. As time has passed, the community reserve of available spiritual capital has noticeably declined. Some question whether younger generations will have the moral fortitude to deal with the difficult times that may lie ahead. Alas, the greatest impact may be on younger generations that are still defining themselves and on those yet to come.

Values, Virtues, and Staying Connected to Our Creator

Since the beginning of the new millennium, a good number of our institutions have left us feeling uneasy, and there are growing concerns about our long-term economic environment. Shortly after 9/11, the Social Security surplus vanished and the national debt clock began ticking again.

Because of challenging economic conditions and defense situations, trade and budget deficits, unfortunately, have reached near-record highs. The federal budget proposal shows hundreds of billions of dollars in annual deficits until 2008, including $455 billion for 2003 and $475 billion for 2004. Furthermore, Congress, unlike it did during both World War II and the Korean War, has failed to adequately cut nondefense discretionary spending in these trying times. Geopolitical tensions and the lingering threat of terrorism have dampened consumer confidence as well, while the labor market tries to recuperate from its worst slump since WWII. And finally, the states are facing their worst monetary demands since the Depression, due primarily to poor fiscal management.

Many people are anxious that they will not have enough assets to be able to retire. With many of the oldest Baby Boomers planning to retire within the next few years, Alan Greenspan recently warned that increasing budget deficits could lead to major funding problems for Social Security and healthcare in the future. Some are worried that our institutions are no longer trustworthy. Still others fear our world is no longer a safe place to live, as the War Against Terrorism continues.

At this critical juncture in our nation's history there is an immense need for more high-caliber leaders. We also need more ordinary heroes from everyday life—those who will help pave America's way to a promising future.

Perhaps Retirees, as elders and counselors, may have a special part yet to play in shaping America's future. These traditional roles, so essential to our nation's beginning, have almost been forsaken. To a large degree, our world reveres those who are young and successful. Unfortunately, it often ignores the wisdom of Retirees who have prevailed in facing the challenges of the past.

It feels good to hear the President say that the state of our Union has never been stronger, and Lee Greenwood's performance of "God Bless the U.S.A." is inspirational. Nevertheless, the strength of our Union and the foundation of the American Dream rest squarely on values, virtues, and staying connected to our Creator—not just on a pot of gold at the end of the rainbow.

"Intoxicated with unbroken success, we have become too self-sufficient to feel the necessity of redeeming and preserving grace; too proud to pray to the God that made us."

—Abraham Lincoln

Chapter 13

Return to the City of God

*"The wall of separation between
church and state needs to be a porous one that allows
reasonable accommodation between the two."*
—Charlie Douglas—

In St. Augustine's classic, *City of God,* he says there are two kinds of "cities." The earthly city, or City of Man, sets forth the notion that life on Earth is temporal. In this city, obtaining power, acquiring possessions, and building vast empires are the things sought after. The American Dream for the City of Man revolves around the domain of the state, political authority, and what people possess.

The City of God, on the other hand, sees following God's will as the highest purpose, all people as brothers and sisters, and eternal life as the primary goal. How gifts and talents are used to transform the temporal world in order to build God's kingdom, above all, describes this city and, accordingly, defines the American Dream.

In the early fifth century, as Rome was perishing, Augustine's work describing these dualistic cities made it clear that as man's world passes away there was another, more enduring world, which was more essential. Few literary works have had a greater impact on the development of Western civilization.

These two "cities" naturally have very different understandings of the purpose of life, the role of God, and the necessity of virtues. Unfortunately, our culture today more closely resembles a City of Man, even though America began as a City of God. Early settlers were devoted to their religious faiths and virtuous conduct. Although religion and our federal legislature were to be separated, our limited government was designed so its people and their Creator would stay united.

Our Creator and Our Unalienable Rights

Our Declaration of Independence, principally drafted by Thomas Jefferson, refers to our Creator, directly and indirectly, four different times, and clearly states—"All Men are created equal, that they are endowed by their Creator with certain unalienable Rights, that among these are Life, Liberty, and the pursuit of Happiness. That to secure these rights, Governments are instituted among men...." These rights, as given to us by our Creator, were the very truths that the Founding Fathers in the Declaration of Independence held to be self-evident.

It was never the framers' intentions that individuals had unalienable rights in and of themselves, or that the government possessed its power to govern independent of our Creator. Clearly, the Declaration of Independence embraced the notion that God alone gave us our unalienable rights, and the primary purpose of government was to secure those God-given rights. The Constitution does not grant us any rights; it simply guarantees them.

America's government was unique because it was established with the understanding that God does not choose select groups or certain families to rule. Our newly established republic decisively rejected the Divine Right which many monarchies had used for centuries to justify their rule. The Divine Right of kings and queens long held that their power came to them directly from God, which they in turn used in governing the people.

Our limited form of government, on the other hand, adopted the Transmission Theory, whereby God's authority is not transmitted directly to those who rule, but indirectly to them through the people. Under this theory, power came unswervingly from God to the people who, in turn, loaned it to the government. The government is, therefore, supposed to reflect godly principles.

Today, regrettably, many of us see little or no connection between our faiths and our country's future. We have outlawed any meaningful existence of the Creator, prayer, and many of our religious traditions and customs in our public institutions.

School children can apparently feel good about showing off their latest toys during "Show and Tell" sessions, but must hide their faith within, as if it is something embarrassing. Even academically, they are rarely learning about each other's faiths. Unfortunately, this precludes them from respecting differences and celebrating common interests.

Our children need to be receiving an ample amount of information regarding their moral heritage through school history, but they are not getting it. In the past, textbooks like *The New England Primer* and, thereafter, *The McGuffey Readers,* although not politically correct because they espoused only a Protestant-Christian religion, nevertheless, imparted an education rich in convictions, principles, and moral excellence for well over 200 years.

Similarly, many of the first colleges and universities like Harvard, Yale, and Princeton were founded for the purpose of teaching students about the Creator and all of creation. Today, not one of America's 50 top colleges and universities requires students to study American history. The role of religion in the history of the United States has essentially been forgotten.

For the majority of our nation's history, school teachers also played an important role as character educators. Yet, during the 1960s and 1970s, they became facilitators as students were encouraged to clarify their own values. This mindset has continued unaltered today as student values are radically influenced by television, hit movies, the Internet, and pop records.

Eminem, the foul-mouthed rap artist, is a very powerful name in music, who exerts a tremendous influence on today's youth. Far from being a healthy role model, Eminem's lyrics are often racist, sexist, and otherwise offensive. President Bush referred to him as "the most dangerous threat to American children since polio."

In school, sex education is mandatory while religious education is frowned upon. But, as distinguished author and social policy commentator Michael Novak pointed out, "Americans are starved for good conversations about important matters of the human spirit. In Victorian England, religious devotion was not a forbidden topic of conversation; sex was. In America today, the inhibitions are reversed."

Freedom *From* Religion as Church and State Separate

The framers of our Constitution plainly wanted to safeguard our federal government from adopting a national religion and prohibit giving preferential treatment to particular religious sects or denominations. But, in our concern over "separating church from state" we have, in some cases, extended preferential treatment to those who would *prevent* the practicing of religion at the expense of it being freely exercised.

This fact can be seen from reviewing the *Annals of Congress* where James Madison initially proposed the following religion clause regarding the First Amendment—"The civil rights of none shall be abridged on account of religious belief or worship, nor shall any *national* religion be established, nor shall the full and equal rights of conscience be in any manner, or on any pretext, infringed."

Madison believed people feared one religious sect might obtain preeminence, or that two may join together and establish a national religion to which they would compel others to conform. Madison ultimately withdrew the word "national," though, because others objected that the Constitution created only a limited federal government, not a national government.

Our country's founders wanted to prevent the type of religious persecution that had occurred in parts of Europe from happening in America. Americans, however, were always supposed to have the religious freedom to openly pursue God in their state and local communities. Religious tolerance, as opposed to religious abstinence, was seen as necessary for the proper functioning of society.

At the time our Constitution was created, relationships between religion and civil governments were defined in most state constitutions and local charters. Our "limited federal government," which was instituted primarily for military protection and, secondarily, to foster interstate commerce, generally did not encroach upon the states' jurisdictions.

Our Constitution essentially provided enumerated powers to a limited federal government, and religion was not one of the powers given to Congress. That is why the original Constitution reveals little regarding religion.

The Library of Congress's highly acclaimed exhibit on "Religion and the Founding of the American Republic" by Dr. James H. Hutson, which can be found at www.loc.gov/exhibits/religion/, makes this point regarding the Constitution's relative silence on religion—"That religion was not otherwise addressed in the Constitution did not make it an 'irreligious' document any more than the Articles of Confederation was an irreligious document. The Constitution dealt with the church precisely as the Articles had, thereby maintaining, at the national level, the religious status quo. In neither document did the people yield any explicit power to act in the field of religion. But the absence of expressed powers did not prevent either the Continental-Confederation Congress or the Congress under the Constitution from sponsoring a program to support general, nonsectarian religion."

The Constitution was not meant to replace existing state constitutions; it was created primarily to establish limits on the powers of a new federal government. The First Amendment of The Bill of Rights clearly reflects this since only "*Congress* shall make no law respecting an establishment of religion or prohibiting the free exercise thereof." State governments had no such restrictions. More importantly, they would not have ratified the Constitution and The Bill of Rights if they had understood that this would dismantle religious expression in public institutions within each state.

The Constitution simply deferred to the states on matters of religion. However, this didn't mean that the people of all religious faiths within any state were treated equally. Rather, some states like Massachusetts and Virginia, adopted state religions. Furthermore, when state constitutions adopted a bill of rights that promised religious freedom to individuals, most "religious freedom" was tied to professing some form of Christianity.

In this regard, the efforts of Thomas Jefferson and James Madison were instrumental in establishing religious freedom in their own state of Virginia—a standard other states soon began to endorse. Virginia, like other states at the time, was supporting religion through a general religious tax. Taxpayers earmarked which church they wanted to support. Yet, this resulted in only

Christian churches being supported, where already-established churches became even stronger. Madison's *Memorial and Remonstrance Against Religious Assessments* and Jefferson's *Statute for Religious Freedom,* thwarted state aid to religion in Virginia and established religious liberty.

As you may surmise, no Moslems or Hindus gave their input into drafting our nation's founding documents. Be that as it may, all people in America today—not just Christians—are entitled to an appropriate expression of their religious beliefs.

There are those who label the call for religious principles and virtues in the public arena as coming only from the "religious right," which they claim espouses "fundamental Christianity" alone. Yet, our Government needs to accommodate the active participation of people from all faiths. It's important to keep in mind that, in our pluralistic society, republican virtue rests on more than any one religion.

For people like Barry Lynn of Americans United for the Separation of Church and State, however, there is no room even for the expression of religious principles in our public arena. In the spring of 2003, Secretary of Education Rod Paige made the following comment: "All things equal, I would prefer to have a child in a school that has a strong appreciation for the *values* of the Christian Community, where a child is taught to have a strong faith. Where a child is taught that there is a source of strength greater than themselves."

Lynn issued a call for Paige to repudiate his comments or resign, even though Paige, in his unofficial statement of personal preference, said nothing about teaching Christian theology in our public schools—only *values* of the Christian community.

In no event should there be an "impenetrable wall" separating church and state precisely because it prevents sensible and limited expressions of religion in our public institutions. It also abandons vital customs and traditions that are part of our moral heritage. Even Jefferson and Madison, during their presidencies, encouraged and attended the largest Protestant church services in America, which were held at the Capitol beginning in 1800 and continued there over the next 50 years.

Today, staying connected to our Creator, regrettably, has little place left in our public domain. This is true despite the fact that, according to a recent *Newsweek* poll, most Americans believe it is acceptable for the government to promote religious expression, as long as no specific religion is mentioned.

Although Congress still has no law respecting the establishment of religion, our laws often publicly prohibit its free exercise. Recently, a teacher's aide was suspended from her job for a year without pay for refusing to remove a small cross necklace. She took formal legal action in response, and believes that religion is "systematically being removed from society."

Instead of freedom of religion, we more often have freedom *from* religion. Yet the relationship between religion and government in the United States should only prevent the government from establishing a religion. It's important to note that it should always protect privately initiated religious expressions and activities from government interference and discrimination. Efforts to separate "church from state" should under no circumstances separate God from country and its citizens.

Are We Still "One Nation Under God"?

Around the start of the Baby Boom, the Supreme Court in *Everson v. Board of Education* (1947) essentially rewrote the First Amendment to say "Congress [and all States] shall make no law regarding the establishment of religion...." The Court's decision in that case made a de facto amendment to our Constitution, something which Congress was never able to accomplish.

The rationale for the Court's decision in *Everson* was to link the First Amendment and Fourteenth Amendment together, but this was not the intent of the authors of the First and Fourteenth Amendments. The First Amendment, along with the other nine Amendments to the Constitution that comprise The Bill of Rights, was originally intended as a limitation on the federal government's action against the citizens of individual states. However, during the twentieth century, the Supreme Court began using the Fourteenth Amendment (adopted in 1868), which was initially enacted to extend civil rights to freed slaves, to also limit the actions of state and local governments.

In *Everson,* the Court, in making its unprecedented ruling, reflected the religious atrocities that had been committed against minorities in Europe during World War II by totalitarian governments. America's government, on the other hand, was much more egalitarian and the Court now provided demonstrable evidence of that. As such, the Court began ignoring the religious sentiment of the majority of Americans. For the first time in its 150-year history, it began finding that the Establishment Clause of the First Amendment was intended to erect a "wall of separation" between church and state.

During the Baby Boom and Generation X, the Court built the wall higher and made it more impenetrable. States were no longer permitted to have nonobligatory nondenominational prayers recited in public schools, nor could they set aside one minute of the day for silent voluntary prayer. They weren't even allowed to have the Ten Commandments posted in public classrooms.

Recently, the Ninth U.S. Circuit Court of Appeals found that the phrase "One nation under God," as uttered by public school teachers leading school children in the Pledge of Allegiance, was unconstitutional under the Establishment Clause. Pathetically, pledging allegiance to our nation's flag "under God" may no longer be legally permissible in our public school systems under the First Amendment. Yet, burning the flag as an act of insurrection receives Constitutional protection under the same amendment as "freedom of speech."

The dispiriting truth is that we are no longer free to publicly pursue God in our local communities as our Founding Fathers had originally intended and put into practice for over 150 years. C.S. Lewis noted that "the modern world insists that religion be a purely private affair, then shrinks the area of privacy to the vanishing point. When the state moves in, separation means forcing the church to move out. And the state keeps moving into new domains that it claims as its own."

America, however, was founded upon godly principles, and religious faith played an important role in our nation's history. If you have any doubts, just consider the following.

The Continental Confederation of Congress

The Continental Confederation of Congress governed the United States from 1774 to 1789, with many of its members divided by differing state interests and various religious faiths. At their first meeting, there was rumor of an impending war with Britain, which had the most powerful army and largest navy in the world. So what was the new Congress's first official act? Members requested a session of prayer.

Some initially objected because the many differing religious groups (Episcopalians, Quakers, Anabaptists, Presbyterians, Deists, and Congregationalists) present would not allow them to join in the same act of prayer. Yet, they quickly put their differences aside and found common ground in piety, virtue, and patriotism as they read a Jewish prayer, Psalm 35, in *The Book of Common Prayer*.

John Adams, who attended the meeting, wrote his wife Abigail, "I never saw a greater effect upon an audience. It seemed as if heaven had ordained that Psalm be read on that morning. It was enough to melt a stone. I saw tears gush into the eyes of the old, grave pacific Quakers of Philadelphia. I must beg you, Abigail, to read that Psalm."

The Articles of Confederation did not officially authorize its members to become involved in religious affairs. Nevertheless, Congress appointed Congressional chaplains, sponsored the publication of the Bible, and proclaimed national days of thanksgiving, humiliation, fasting, and prayer at least twice a year throughout the war—beseeching God to establish "the independence of these United States upon the basis of religion and virtue."

They also passed the Northwest Ordinance in 1787 for establishing new territories northwest of the Ohio River. It contained the following language: "Religion, morality, and knowledge being necessary to good government and the happiness of mankind, schools and the means of education shall be forever encouraged." Americans did not disapprove of their actions. Early legislatures saw little danger of "an establishment of religion" where no preference was extended to any particular denomination, and where the outlays of funds were one-time grants or involved only modest amounts.

George Washington

George Washington believed in the importance of religious principles for the new republican government. As Commander-in-chief, Washington had his troops begin each day in public prayer. His first official act after being sworn in as President was to join with all the members of the House and Senate in a two-hour worship service. Furthermore, it was George Washington who warned all in his Farewell Address:

"Of all the dispositions and habits which lead to political prosperity, *religion and morality are indispensable supports....* And let us with caution indulge the supposition that morality can be maintained without religion. Whatever may be conceded to the influence of refined education on minds of peculiar structure, reason and experience both forbid us to expect that national morality can prevail in exclusion of religious principle."

Benjamin Franklin

Though widely known as a deist, Benjamin Franklin acknowledged the need for prayer within government during the Continental Convention on June 28, 1787. At 81, he addressed George Washington, the Convention's President, as follows: "In the beginning of the contest with Great Britain when we were sensible to danger, we had daily prayers in this room for Divine protection.

"Our prayers, Sir, were heard and they were graciously answered.... I have lived, Sir, a long time and the longer I live, the more convincing proofs I see of this truth that—*God governs in the affairs of men.* And, if a sparrow cannot fall to the ground without His notice, is it probable that an empire can rise without His aide?

"We have been assured, Sir, in the Sacred Writings that, 'except the Lord build the house, they labor in vain that build it.' ...I firmly believe this; and I also believe that without His concurring aid we shall succeed in this political building no better than the Builders of Babel.... I therefore beg leave to move that henceforth, prayers imploring the assistance of Heaven and its blessing on our deliberation be held in this

Assembly every morning before we proceed to business, and that one or more of the Clergy of this City be requested to officiate in that Service."

John Adams

For many years, our nation's second President, John Adams, made it a practice to annually read through the entire Bible, and routinely stressed the importance of biblically based principles in government. On October 11, 1798, he addressed the military as follows: "We have no government armed with power capable of contending with human passions unbridled by morality and religion. Avarice, ambition, revenge, or gallantry would break the strongest cords of our Constitution as a whale goes thorough a net. Our Constitution was made only for a moral and religious people. It is wholly inadequate to the government of any other."

And in a letter to Benjamin Rush, dated August 28, 1811, Adams noted that *"religion and virtue are the only foundations, not only of republicanism and of all free government, but of social felicity under all governments and in all the combinations of human society."*

Alexis de Tocqueville

This French philosopher wrote the acclaimed, *Democracy in America*, a two-volume study of the American people and their political institutions.

In his writings, de Tocqueville notes that, "I sought the key to the greatness of America.... Not until I went into the churches of America and heard her pulpits flame with righteousness did I understand the secret of her genius and power. *America is great because America is good*, and if America ever ceases to be good, America will cease to be great....

"Religion in America takes no direct part in their government of society, but it must be regarded as the first of their political institutions. I do not know whether all Americans have a sincere faith in their religion—for who can search the human heart? But I am certain that they hold it [religion] to be indispensable to the maintenance of republic institutions."

Gouverneur Morris

A signatory to the Constitution, Gouverneur Morris spoke more than any other member from the floor of the Constitutional Convention. He was also head of the committee responsible for the final wording of the Constitution. In a letter to Lord George Gordon on June 28, 1792, Morris said, "I believe that *religion is the only solid base of morals* and that morals are the only possible support of free governments."

Abraham Lincoln

Abraham Lincoln, the sixteenth President of the United States, demonstrated great courage by risking the nation for the sake of liberty. When he gave The Gettysburg Address he said, "...that *this nation under God* shall have freedom, and that government of the people, by the people, for the people shall not perish from the earth."

But did you also know that in a Presidential proclamation made on March 30, 1863 Lincoln established a National Fast Day? He stated, "We have grown in numbers, wealth, and power as no other nation has ever grown. But we have forgotten God. We have forgotten the gracious hand which preserves us in peace, and multiplied and enriched and strengthened us; as we have vainly imagined, in the deceitfulness of our hearts, that all these blessings were produced by some superior wisdom and virtue of our own.

"Intoxicated with unbroken success we have become too self-sufficient to feel the necessity of redeeming and preserving grace; too proud to pray to the God that made us. It behooves us then to humble ourselves before the offended power to confess our national sins and to pray for clemency and forgiveness."

"In God We Trust"—*The Foundation of Our Nation's Strength*

Our nation's motto, "In God We Trust," was originally placed on United States' coins beginning in 1864 largely because of the increased religious sentiment that existed during the Civil War. At that time, the Secretary of the Treasury received many appeals from people throughout the country, urging that the government recognize the Deity on U.S. coins. It was believed that no reasonable citizen could object to "In God We Trust" since we openly claimed "divine protection."

Church of Holy Trinity v. United States (1892)

This Supreme Court decision emphatically declared that history clearly demonstrates that the American people are a religious people. This was shown by the religious objects described by the original grants and charters of the colonies, and the recognition of religion in the most solemn acts of their history. It was also displayed in the constitutions of the states and that of the nation.

Over the last 55 years, our courts, in many cases, have been legislating against a reasonable accommodation of religious expression. At this time, almost all references to God and religion are prohibited in our public institutions. Civil laws, particularly those regulating marriage, are no longer reflective of biblical morality as so often has been the case throughout American law.

Ironically, there is now more religious correctness under the guise of "ceremonial deism" allowed in our federal institutions than in our state institutions. For example, both houses of Congress begin each day with prayer by clergy appointed by official chaplains and paid from the Treasury of the United States. Likewise, the Supreme Court opens each session with an invocation for Divine protection—"God save the United States and the Honorable Court." Public schools, on the other hand, are forbidden to have even one minute devoted to non-mandatory silent prayer.

The Ten Commandments appear on the wall above the head of the Chief Justice in the Supreme Court, while public schools are forbidden to even inconspicuously post a copy of them on a bulletin board. Every President of the United States has placed his hand on the *Bible* and asked for God's protection upon taking office, whereas the *Bible* is not to be called upon in many of our public institutions.

America's heritage is interwoven with God and religious convictions, but, sadly, this part of history is no longer found in our textbooks. The state and our institutions don't need to adopt formal religion to become better, so much as they need to embrace the virtues of religion and the principles of a loving God.

The Supreme Court in Zorach v. Clauson (1952) said, "We are a religious people and our institutions presuppose a Supreme Being." Today, it is still plain to see that America is not an irreligious nation, but a multi-faith nation of religious beliefs. The survival of our moral heritage, at least to some extent, depends upon our institutions being allowed to reflect our belief in that Supreme Being.

America need not abandon the significant contributions of Jefferson and Madison toward establishing religious liberty for all people. It is obvious that having close ties between church and state has proven to be a flawed model for government, even in Christendom.

On the other hand, abandoning all sensible ties between church and state, like prohibiting faith-based initiatives, or a noncompulsory pledge of allegiance, or even a moment of silence to permit nonmandatory school prayer, goes too far. The wall of separation between church and state needs to be porous, allowing reasonable accommodation between the two. Even Jefferson asked, "Can the liberties of a nation be so sure when we remove their only firm basis, a conviction in the minds of the people, that these liberties are the gift of God?"

Organized religion by no means offers a panacea. Being an institution maintained by human beings, it suffers from the same imperfections that come with our human condition. As our spirited nation began, for example, religion was used to condone horrendous practices like slavery. It also helped foster divisiveness and discrimination by various states against those who believed tenets not popular with the establishment.

For thousands of years, all around the world, wars have been fought in the name of religion. Even today, escalating tensions between Jews and Muslims are rooted in religious differences. Yet, it's important to note that religious confrontations are most often fought over religious supremacy, not over religious virtues.

Religious virtues, regardless of one's particular faith, need to advance the interests of all. Despite the shortcomings of organized religion, religious faith is a tremendous teacher of virtues, with the

Golden Rule being the most recognized throughout all major religions. Religion, as an institution, helps us distinguish right from wrong, and provides us with a viable platform to work with our Creator in realizing the fullness of the American Dream.

Values Are Not the Same as Virtues

Today, we have almost come to expect differences in values as expressed in the contemporary phrase, "You have your values and I have mine." Values are usually personal and relative, and may have nothing to do with the notion of advancing an objective good.

For example, since Roe v. Wade was decided by the Supreme Court in 1973, we legally protect a woman's right to choose whether or not to have an abortion. In many cases, nonprofit agencies, like Planned Parenthood, which received $240 million in government funds in 2002, assist women in making or carrying out their decisions. Currently, the bitter political fight over abortion divides our nation because people have different opinions and values regarding this controversial issue.

Yet if values are simply a matter of personal preference and none are objectively superior, then stealing, cheating, and lying would presumably be as good as any other conduct. Clearly, not all values are on equal footing. It stands to reason that if there were no values worthy of becoming virtues then we would have no standards by which to make wise choices.

Only values which advance an objective good can serve as the basis for virtuous conduct. Virtues, unlike many values, withstand the test of time. They are habitual and result in a firm disposition to do an objective good. Our Founding Fathers, regardless of their particular beliefs in organized religion, nevertheless, agreed that virtues were indispensable for the maintenance of the republic.

Virtues, as we have come to understand them today, were espoused by Aristotle in the 300s BC. He divided all virtues into those that were moral and affected character, and those that were intellectual and concerned one's thoughts.

Aristotle taught that virtue is a sensible midpoint between two extremes. For example, the virtue of courage is that midpoint between the coward who runs from danger and the reckless individual who blindly rushes ahead into danger. A courageous person, on the other hand, boldly faces up to those appropriate dangers when he or she must.

Christian theologian St. Thomas Aquinas, thereafter grouped four key virtues together as the cardinal virtues: justice (fairness), prudence (wisdom), fortitude (moral courage), and temperance (moderation). Faith, hope, and charity subsequently became known as the theological virtues for Christians, with the greatest of these being charity.

Benjamin Franklin believed that there were thirteen virtues necessary for true success: temperance, silence, order, resolution, frugality, industry, sincerity, justice, moderation, cleanliness, tranquility, chastity, and humility.

Several years ago, in *The Book of Virtues,* William J. Bennett promoted ten virtues: self-discipline, compassion, responsibility, friendship, work, courage, perseverance, honesty, loyalty, and faith.

As we clarify our own core values, we need to do so within the context of non-economic assets and religious virtues. But virtues should not be imposed on anyone by a restrictive list. They need to be discerned in accordance with the dictates of one's conscience, to the degree that they help advance an objective good. Virtues, regardless of whether or not they are part of a comprehensive list, by their very nature keep us connected to the source and supply of all love.

If we are to responsibly move forward as a nation and realize the fullness of the American Dream, we need to look earnestly to our Creator to help us recast our country into a City of God. The task may appear to be daunting, but we would do well not to bet against a Creator who lovingly aligned the planets and the stars in the sky.

C.S. Lewis believed that the evidence for God's existence lies all around us. He said, "We may ignore but we can nowhere evade the presence of God. The world is crowded with Him. He walks everywhere incognito. And the incognito is not always easy to penetrate. The real labor is to remember to attend. In fact to come awake. Still more to remain awake."

"**M**any have painstakingly climbed the ladder of success rung by rung—the diploma, the late nights, the promotions—only to discover as they reached the top, that their ladder of success was leaning against the wrong wall."

—Dr. Stephen Covey

Chapter 14

Commit to Climbing God's Ladder First

"If our attachment to material wealth or worldly matters becomes more important than our desire for God, we can be sure our ladder is leaning against the wrong wall."
—Charlie Douglas—

We make many choices every day. Ultimately, our decisions dictate the ladders we spend our precious life's energy trying to climb. It is rare to write down goals. But it is rarer still to think them through in terms of their overall contribution toward our mission to love our Creator and one another. Many of us go through life letting the media, advertisers, and others' opinions determine what we should value and how we ought to behave.

To be sure, there are times when we demonstrate our goodness and love for our neighbors. The problem is, however, that loving God and our neighbors is frequently no longer our primary focus. We are more likely to value possessions and accomplishments over prayer and people. Many have replaced love-centered values with secular ones, spiritual capital with financial capital.

Be that as it may, we are designed primarily to be nurtured by immortal love—not just for the temporary gratification that the material world offers. At times, we may even cry out for God's love to fill us up, but fail to notice we have already filled ourselves with worldly concerns. It is ironic how job titles, money, and other worldly achievements do not seem to have enough vigor to keep us fulfilled for long. We have placed more meaning in temporal affairs than they were meant to have.

Seek Spiritual Development—*God Hasn't Changed*

Several years ago, while riding on a tour bus during a vacation in Greece, I was awed by what humanity had been able to accomplish so many years ago. From the architectural genius of the Acropolis in Athens to the scholarly writings of men like Aristotle and Plato—it was all quite impressive.

It made me wonder whether humanity has really progressed much during the last few thousand years. Sure, we can now do business globally on the information superhighway, but what about our personal and spiritual development?

Our tour guide had been rambling on for quite a while, pointing out one Greek structure after another. It was one of those moments in life when just about the time you are ready to tune somebody out, he or she says something that speaks straight to your heart. She said, "It's funny that the ancient Greeks dedicated their entire lives in service to the gods. They lived life knowing they would only play a small part in the building of a structure which honored a being greater than themselves. Today, we have lost that ancient spirit."

Looking back with the advantage of hindsight, we can see that our expectations of God have, in some cases, changed. For nearly 1,900 years, Christians called upon God predominantly to assist them in their walk toward salvation. Beginning in 1952, however, the groundbreaking international bestseller, *The Power of Positive Thinking* by Dr. Norman Vincent Peale, urged us to call upon God to help us achieve personal happiness and success. The idea was that God should be our partner in business, as well as in all other aspects of our lives.

But is it really the right thing to do to call upon our Creator to be our partner in business, as well as in all other aspects of our lives? Absolutely! We stand more of a chance of being successful in business and in living the American Dream when God is a part of everything we do. Divine inclusion keeps us closer to God, enabling us to better live the dreams our Maker has planted in our hearts. It also enables us to more readily treat others in a compassionate, encouraging, and giving manner. The calamities at Tyco, Enron, and WorldCom would not have happened had the key people truly had God as their business partner.

However, there is a fine line between seeking God's assistance in becoming all that we can be in accordance with God's plan, and seeking to change it to conform to our own personal desires. In some cases, we may be too busy soliciting God about *our* will to be able to discern *God's* will for our lives.

Let Material Success Be Evidence That You Have Given

Is it wrong to be successful and have nice things? There is nothing wrong with worldly success and the material goods that often come along with it. We need to feel good about and be grateful for our accomplishments and the possessions we have. Our worldly accomplishments and acquisitions may be the best evidence that we have been of service to others—and God.

But we also need to ask ourselves, "Why were we created? Was it just to be successful in worldly matters? Or do we need to focus on using our desires, gifts, and talents to spread God's love?"

Once when Mother Teresa was visiting the United States, a Senator asked her, "In India where there are so many problems, can you ever be successful at what you do—isn't it hopeless to try?" She replied, "Well, Senator, we're not called to always be successful in the eyes of the world, but we are called to be faithful."

Take Notice of Where You Have Placed Your Ladders

We expend our life's energy climbing ladders in pursuit of our goals. But as esteemed author Dr. Stephen Covey points out in his book, *First Things First,* "Many have painstakingly climbed the ladder of success rung by rung—the diploma, the late nights, the promotions—only to discover as they reached the top, that their ladder of success was leaning against the wrong wall." Many of us would do well to investigate, from time to time, on what walls our ladders are resting.

The material-capital worldview tells us that our accomplishments and possessions are how we should measure our intrinsic worth. Yet a spiritual-capital mindset reveals that how well we live out godly principles and selfless values needs to be the final word on how successfully we have each answered our life's call.

Culturally, many of us continue to move away from traditional religious institutions as we search for the truth. Of those who have stayed, some believe that going to their places of worship is all that they need to do to be faithful. But sitting in our places of worship and waiting for our one-hour obligation to be over, does not make us any more spiritual than attending Major League baseball games makes us professional ballplayers. Being a spectator alone won't get you in the game.

A better indication of our faithfulness may be found when we periodically review our checkbooks, daily planners, or Personal Digital Assistants (PDAs). Ask yourself this: "If I lost my checkbook, daily planner, or PDA and a stranger picked them up, would that individual be able to see evidence of the person I believe myself to be?"

Success Comes in Reaching for Yet Another Rung

We continue to fall short, time and time again, in our efforts to love and serve our Creator, no matter how faithful we vow or endeavor to become. Many of us will still spend most of our days straddling the fence between God's ladder and the material-world ladder. Our personal success, however, should not be measured by how far up God's ladder we climb. Rather, it could best be found in the *courage* by which we reach for yet another rung. As C.S. Lewis wrote, "Virtue—even attempted virtue—brings light; indulgence brings fog."

It is a real challenge putting Godly principles first, while living in a world where we need to make money. It has always been a challenge, even for those who are later looked upon as saints. Most of us are not called to be a St. Francis or a Mother Teresa, and thereby live in a state of poverty in order to serve God. On the contrary, the majority of us have also been entrusted with the responsibility of putting food on our tables and roofs over our families' heads.

Poverty Itself Is Not a Virtue—*Even Jesus Received Financial Aid*

Material wealth is not a bad thing. There is nothing holy about debt, or not being able to pay your bills, or an economy that has run out of money. In many ways, we can financially serve the poor better by not allowing ourselves to become one of them.

There is nothing virtuous about poverty itself. Poverty alone has no intrinsic goodness. Only the motive behind poverty may be virtuous if the desire is to help remove the obstacles which stand in the way of working toward spiritual perfection. But material wealth can support a quite holy effort—depending on how it is accumulated and used.

Jesus did not condemn the possession of worldly goods or even of great wealth. Some of His friends were financially well-off. In fact, as explained in Luke 8:1-3, several Galilean women who followed Jesus aided Him considerably in His ministry with their financial resources. These women, who had practically no standing in society, helped sustain Jesus and His twelve disciples with their monetary contributions. Jesus, however, continually warned about the dangers of being *attached* to riches. Attachment to riches hinders our ability to love.

The challenge is not that money itself prevents us from climbing God's ladder first. Money is just a medium of exchange. The greater concern is that many of us do not suspect that we are spending the majority of our time climbing ladders that rest on walls belonging only to the material world.

If our attachment to material wealth or worldly matters becomes more important than our desire for God, our ladders are leaning against the wrong wall. Lest we forget, the decline of many great civilizations began not so much by their failure to choose "the better walls," but in their unresponsiveness as to which walls would lead to better places.

"The Soviet Union is suffering from a spiritual decline. We were among the last to understand that in the age of information technology the most valuable asset is knowledge, which springs from individual imagination and creativity. We will pay for our mistakes for many years to come."

—Mikhail Gorbachev

Chapter 15

Pursue Godly Dependence Before Financial Independence

*"Financial independence can be a
wonderful blessing if it fosters the development of
one's talents and the pursuit of worthy causes."*
—Charlie Douglas—

It is human nature to want independence. As babies we first struggle to crawl, then walk. We fall many times in the process, but in our efforts to stand on our own two feet we remain undaunted. Later, we strive to become independent of our parents and our surroundings, as we continue to nurture our own sense of autonomy. Innately, we yearn to have no masters over us.

America is increasingly emphasizing the development of the individual, which may come at the expense of the community. Self-determination, self-fulfillment, and self-sufficiency are sometimes valued more today than teamwork, fidelity, and altruism.

In recent years, one area that is particularly alluring is seeking financial independence. This can be a noble pursuit, provided we put our Creator first in the process. And in some ways, it's easier to focus on helping our neighbors when we are in a position to pay our monthly bills.

Our Latest Expression of the Desire for Freedom

The August 1999 edition of *The Wall Street Journal* magazine, *Smart Money,* featured a cover which boldly stated: RETIRE TEN YEARS EARLY—It's America's newest obsession! A gentleman from New York responded in a follow-up letter to the editor, "What's next? How to retire in your senior year of high school? I would like to see one—just one—article on money management for people who would like to continue to contribute, in addition to remaining active and mentally alert."

There are obviously many ways to contribute. And, depending on what we wish to accomplish, financial independence can give us the time and money to continue to pursue God's dreams for us more fully.

While most of today's Retirees may have thought little during their youth about one day achieving financial independence, younger generations are pursuing this newest obsession with great fervor. At the end of the previous millennium, a survey of college juniors and seniors revealed that most thought they would retire between the ages of 40 and 50. Financial independence is becoming the latest expression of our yearning to be free.

In many cases, it is a freedom born out of responsible planning and discipline. Financial independence can also be a wonderful blessing if it fosters the development of our talents and the pursuit of worthy causes. However, it is only beneficial when it leads us toward our Creator and inspires growth in non-economic assets.

In the New Testament, Jesus instructed the 12 apostles to go forth and continue His mission. He further commanded them to take nothing for the journey—no food, no sack, and no money in their belts. His instructions seem so contrary to how we live life today. Yet Jesus was not overly concerned that His disciples might incur physical inconveniences during their journeys. He wanted them to always be conscious of their dependence on God for everything.

Deuteronomy 8:18 says, "Thou shalt remember the Lord thy God: for it is He that giveth thee power to get wealth." Do we acknowledge and thank our Creator for whatever prosperity has been entrusted to us? Are we humble about it, or do we have the attitude that we did it all on our own? Do we label ourselves "self-made" when we are really "Creator-made"?

As we seek to answer these questions, we recognize that our economic world today is vastly different from what it was when the *Bible* was written, or even when the American Dream came into being. We no longer live in an agrarian society when small communities were relatively self-contained and people worked the land together to provide for life's basic needs. Today, our needs are met through a global marketplace. Food products can now be conveniently delivered to our homes by the simple click of a mouse. As our world has advanced, there are many positive financial benefits passed on to others when we pursue our self-interests under capitalism.

Be Rich by Being Resourceful

After America declared its independence from Britain, political economist and philosopher Adam Smith, author of *The Wealth of Nations,* promoted the idea that government needs to let the market be, with little or no regulation. He described how the unfettered pursuit by individuals of their own self-interests led directly to the increased well-being of the larger society. Smith observed that an "invisible hand" guided the unintended actions of individuals toward increased societal wealth.

More recently, in the book *God Wants You to Be Rich* by Paul Zane Pilzer, the author builds upon Smith's observations by telling us that God wants all of us to increase our individual wealth because this almost always results in an even larger increase in societal wealth.

Traditionally, economists defined wealth as being limited to those well-to-do individuals who stockpiled as much of a given natural resource as possible. They depended exclusively on the natural resources that God deposited on the earth, consuming or amassing what they found, then moving on to find more. The thinking of the day suggested that the more resources one put aside for him or herself, the wealthier that person became since there was less available for others.

Today, the synergism of technology can expand the natural resources that currently exist. Consider the American farmer, for example. In 1930, there were 30 million farmers barely producing enough to feed 100 million people. By 1980, however, there were 3 million farmers producing enough to feed over 300 million people.

Currently, the major part of our economy is involved in producing innovative products and services that did not exist when the twentieth century began. And the most precious resource available to us is not found in the earth, but in our abilities to innovate and be resourceful.

Pope John Paul II commented on the importance of our resourcefulness as follows: "Whereas at one time the decisive factor of production was the land, today the decisive factor is increasingly man himself, that is, his knowledge, especially his scientific knowledge, his capacity for interrelated and compact originations, as well as his ability to perceive the needs of others and to satisfy them."

Every man and woman has been created in the image of the Creator, and each of us helps co-create the future of the world. As such, each of us is endowed with an unalienable responsibility to create with reverence for human dignity.

Let Desire Be a Positive Motivator

Human beings desire far more than they need. People, unlike other creatures, do not stop when their primary needs have been met. Although our basic needs are few, our desires are often never ending.

Fortunately, this has motivated many to employ their gifts and talents to create resourcefully. In many ways it is because of our capitalistic economy and an ever-increasing consumer demand that we have the incentive to invent new and better ways of doing things. As amazing as it may seem, no matter how much we may earn or possess, most of us can think of things that we would still like to purchase.

Socialism and the community of goods concept failed precisely because there was no economic incentive to develop one's gifts and talents. Without private ownership and the ability to make a profit, creative innovation within the Soviet Union remained suppressed. Former Soviet Union leader Mikhail Gorbachev wisely recognized this when he said: "The Soviet Union is suffering from a spiritual decline. We were among the last to understand that in the age of information technology the most valuable asset is knowledge, which springs from individual imagination and creativity. We will pay for our mistakes for many years to come."

The pursuit of the American Dream through capitalism, on the other hand, continues to spur the improvement and modernization of our goods and services. Our vigorous consumer demand is the primary reason that there is more than one of the same type of product in our households today. Consider that 50 years ago most families had only one television, car, and phone. But now most homes have at least two or more of each.

Moreover, we keep demanding better quality of the same product. For example, we traded in our small black-and-white televisions for color ones, small color televisions for consoles, and consoles for big-screen TVs. Today, big-screen televisions are being exchanged for even bigger screens that have clearer, digital pictures.

The point is that as long as technology keeps advancing, the demand for greater quality will never be satisfied, and the list of what constitutes "necessities" will keep growing. As John Kenneth Galbraith noted in 1958 in his book *The Affluent Society,* "No sharp distinction can be made between luxuries and necessities as societal wealth increases."

Our current preoccupation with consuming and acquiring more, however, has blurred our ability to clearly see what our true needs really are. Note that 95 percent of all of the items demanded by consumers today are in excess of their most basic needs.

Money Is a Tool—*Not a Magic Elixir*

Today, financial independence is pursued as if it were a way of obtaining lifelong emotional security or some type of immunization against the problems of life. But economic freedom is only one component of human freedom, and it is our attachment to money that causes us to feel insecure no matter how much of it we may have. When we equate happiness with material gain, we never seem to achieve enough to keep us happy for long. Benjamin Franklin wrote, "Money never made man happy, nor will it. There is nothing in its nature to produce happiness. The more a man has, the more he wants. Instead of filling a vacuum, it makes one."

Any "happiness" surrounding money is relative and not absolute; it is temporary, not lasting. Oxford University psychologist Michael Argyle, in his comprehensive work *The Psychology of Happiness* observed, "There is very little difference in the levels of reported happiness found in rich and very poor countries. Although the upper classes in any society are somewhat more satisfied with their lives than the lower classes are, the upper classes of rich countries are no more satisfied than the upper classes of much poorer countries. The conditions of life which really make a difference to happiness are those covered by three sources—social relations, work, and leisure. The establishment of a satisfying state of affairs in these spheres does not depend upon money, either absolute or relative."

The real emotional victories in life will never be won with money. True joy comes only from within and is rooted in our loving, caring, and faithful spirits. The tenth century ruler of Cordova, Abd-Al-Rahman, had this to say: "I have now reigned above 50 years in victory or peace, beloved by my subjects, dreaded by my enemies, respected by my allies. Riches and honors, power and pleasure, have awaited my call; nor does any earthly blessing seem to have been wanting.... I have diligently numbered the days of pure and genuine happiness that have fallen to my lot; they amount to 14."

In one sense, if we have enough money to pay our bills and take care of most of our needs, then we have about as much security from money as it was intended to give. To be sure, there is real satisfaction in knowing that we can pay our own way, or that we can handle life's little financial emergencies as they occur. However, having greater amounts of money doesn't proportionately increase our levels of self-satisfaction.

It is oftentimes true that with greater financial resources we are better positioned to share and effect positive change for the betterment of the world. Nevertheless, unless these resources are shared, financial prosperity may serve only to further distance us from the needs of the people we are called to help.

Security gates and alarm systems, unfortunately, can create an environment where it is difficult to see that the sick, poor, and society's so-called undesirables are our brothers and sisters too. And meaningful change can occur without ever possessing significant financial resources. Notable figures like Dorothy Day, Gandhi, and Mother Teresa brought about considerable change for humanity, yet did so primarily by giving away love.

We live in a society of instant credit, where things, in many cases, seem to come so freely. It is easy, therefore, to forget our need for God and each other. Should we face a sudden crisis or be in particular need, it's amazing how quickly we can go from being a self-sufficient adult, with little need for God or anyone else, to a needy "newborn." Sayings like, "There will always be prayer in school as long as there are tests," and "There are no atheists in fox holes," help illustrate this point. Perhaps that is why many theologians believe that the greatest purpose for human suffering is to cause us to turn to our Creator.

We would do well to listen to the wisdom of Douglas Copeland, a Generation X writer, who wrote: "Now here is my secret: I tell it to you with an openness of heart that I doubt I shall ever achieve again, so I pray that you are near in a quiet room as you hear these words. My secret is that I need God—that I am sick and can no longer make it alone. I need God to help me give because I no longer seem to be capable of giving; to help me be kind, as I no longer seem capable of kindness; to help me love, as I seem beyond being able to love."

"*I am of the opinion that my life belongs to the whole community, and as long as I live it is my privilege to do for it whatever I can. I want to be thoroughly used up when I die. For the harder I work the more I live. I rejoice in life for its own sake. Life is no brief candle to me; it is a sort of splendid torch which I have got a hold of for the moment, and I want to make it burn as brightly as possible before handing it on to future generations.*"

—George Bernard Shaw

Chapter 16

Use Your Gifts and Talents or Lose Them

"To be sure, life will continue to deal unfair cards,
but it will also give us many more winning hands as long
as we selflessly stay in the game."
—Charlie Douglas—

There is a story about a preacher who was driving by an immaculate farm. The fields were beautifully cultivated and abundant with well-cared-for crops. The fences, house, and barn were neat, clean, and freshly painted. A row of fine trees led from the road to the house where there were shaded lawns and flower beds. It was a beautiful sight to behold.

When the farmer working in the field got to the end of the row near the road, the preacher stopped his car and called to him. The preacher said, "God sure blessed you with a beautiful farm." The farmer stopped, thought for a moment, and replied: "Yes, He has, and I am grateful. But you should have seen this place when He had it all to Himself."

God Is the Creator—*You Are Only One of His Junior Partners*

Each one of us has been entrusted with a plot of ground. How we tend our portions of land through our words and deeds has a significant impact on whether our plots will become beautiful farms or barren wastelands. However, when we find ourselves taking all the credit for the things we have earned, we need to realize that none of us created our own existence, our innate abilities, or the many exceptional people who helped us along the way. At best, each of us is only a junior co-creator, but never the Creator alone.

All the blessings the farmer had—his ability to reason, to conceive of the possibilities for the farm, the ability to move his limbs and work the land, and the assistance provided by others— were created and conferred on him by God. Like the farmer, we, too, can nurture the basic assets we were born with, but it is God alone who gave them to us.

Consider the commencement address that President George W. Bush delivered at Yale University in 2001: "When I left here, I didn't have much in the way of a life plan. I knew some people who thought they did. But it turned out that we were all in for ups and downs, most of them unexpected. Life takes its own turns, makes its own demands, writes its own story. And along the way, we start to realize we are not the author."

Share Your Talents and You Will Have Success

Many of us are familiar with the parable in the New Testament where a man who was going on a journey called in his servants to entrust his possessions to them. To one he gave five talents; to another, two; to a third, one—to each according to his ability. Then he went away. The servants who received the most talents used them wisely, each doubling what he had received. But the man who received only one talent was so fearful of losing it that he buried it in the ground.

Eventually, the master returned and settled his accounts with them. He congratulated the two who had doubled their talents and invited them to share in his joy. He also gave both greater responsibilities since they had been faithful in small matters. The man who had received just one talent, however, was chastised for his laziness and considered a useless servant. His talent was taken from him and given to the servant who had the most.

Many of us today are like the last servant. Out of fear, we bury our gifts in darkness, rarely allowing them to be exposed to God's illuminating love. The fear of rejection in reaching for the American Dream, of not being good or lovable enough, is for many of us at times all too real.

As we strive for success, we will most likely fail at certain things along the way, without ever becoming a failure in life.

These so-called failures are simply opportunities to learn and grow. Consider the "failure" that George Bailey believed himself to be in the heartwarming Christmas movie, *It's a Wonderful Life*. He dreamed of traveling the world and becoming a famous architect. Yet life had different plans for George Bailey, and he never left the surroundings of his quaint hometown of Bedford Falls. Nor did he have a job other than working at the modest Bailey Building and Loan.

George Bailey felt that he had also failed his family as a provider. Consumed by his own shortcomings, he believed life was no longer worth living. It took an angel-in-training to show him that, despite having fallen far short of his dreams, George had been given a wonderful gift and had used it wisely.

Throughout his life, George Bailey had unselfishly given of himself and demonstrated a willingness to help his neighbor. It was his selflessness in everyday occurrences that had touched many and made a difference in their lives. As the movie ends, George sees himself as a success because he is surrounded by the great love of his family and friends.

Life Gives Winning Hands to Those Who Keep Playing

Using our gifts and talents does not necessarily mean we are going to achieve extraordinary worldly success, and that's okay. The vast majority of us will never receive a $90 million Nike contract like 18-year-old basketball sensation LeBron James did. And we may never write a #1 bestseller like *The Prayer of Jabez* by Bruce Wilkinson, which has sold over 9 million copies. Furthermore, there are only an exceptional few who have a legitimate chance of becoming the next *American Idol*.

The rest of us "George Baileys" need to have faith. We need to believe that by unselfishly sharing our gifts and talents in the ordinary affairs of everyday life, we will touch others in countless small ways. Each of us can have a life that's wonderful and achieve success where it counts the most. To be sure, life will continue to deal unfair cards, but it will also give us many more winning hands as long as we selflessly stay in the game.

In today's culture, nevertheless, many of us are not content with our God-given talents. We long for those certain qualities that will make us exceptional so we can stand out. We want good looks, athletic and artistic ability, and enough enterprising talents to ensure worldly success. In the process, it's easy to lose touch with our God-given abilities that enable us to fulfill aims that may have nothing to do with the material world. Yet, getting in touch with these innate talents in many cases allows us to explore our true callings and passions.

Each of us has been given gifts by our Creator, although not everyone receives the same gifts, nor are they distributed in equal numbers. Each of us, though, has been entrusted with certain God-given desires or talents when it comes to artistic, social, or enterprising endeavors. For that reason, some of us are more inclined to become engineers or businesspeople, for example, instead of artists or counselors.

The challenge today is that many segments of society continue to encourage us to forsake our inner callings and passions. Instead, they encourage career paths that seem to provide the best opportunities for material success alone. Yet, living the American Dream requires getting in touch with our true, God-given abilities and desires. Our creative energies need to be used in ways that contribute to society and make a positive difference in the world.

Expand Your Definition of Work

Many of us spend much of our life's energy "at work," trying to increase our standard of living and keeping up with the "Joneses" in an effort to impress others. Historically, this is a relatively recent phenomenon. For most of humanity's existence, people worked only a few hours a day for their basic needs. As we moved from agriculture to industrialization, however, work hours increased dramatically. Standards were created that labeled a person as lazy if he or she did not work a 40-hour workweek.

The notion that everyone should have a job began with the Industrial Revolution, and full employment has only been a goal of our government since the Depression. Although our average standard of living has risen dramatically in the last 100 years, we continue to work harder to keep increasing it.

Presently, work is seen as something we do only for money. Money, in fact, appears to be the primary tangible evidence that we have worked. It has become a stored medium of exchange for which we trade our precious time and valuable life energy. And yet, learning is work, raising our children is work, community service is work, and pursuing our callings and passions is work.

Work or job title, nevertheless, is so much a part of our concept of self-worth today. The most popular question after "What is your name?" is "What do you do for a living?" But if work is who we are, then how do we define ourselves when we are no longer working? From what will we derive our self-esteem?

Consider the sentiments of a wealthy inheritor who didn't need to work for a living, as described in *Inheritors and Work—The Search for Purpose*, by Barbara Blouin and Katherine Gibson. The inheritor shares her story of how she found self-esteem while performing community service on a trip to India. During the trip, she visited some of Mother Teresa's missions. She recalls her experience: "I'd walk into a hospital, and a sister would hand me a mop or ask me to bathe a patient. The sisters just let us be a part of their work, and I felt they were working at a deep spiritual level that had much more to do with a contemplative presence than it had to do with fixing up the world. It was for me a process of moving from being special to being ordinary, and coming into that everyday, ordinary kind of process and work.

"The main spiritual question for me has had to do with the sense of separation I have felt between myself and God, and between myself and other people. I knew I needed to heal that estrangement, that sense of separation, and come into wholeness. And work has helped me do that.

"I have had to work through a lot of guilt and shame before I could see the advantages of wealth. Now I'm beginning to feel grateful in ways I couldn't have felt before. Money has given me dream time—time to develop my inner spiritual life. I can have quiet time in the morning or evening. I can take walks. The challenge for me, however, is to bring that inner world into the outer world. You could set me down on a rock and I'd be content forever, but to move out into a relationship with the world—with people and with work—that is the challenge."

More important than enabling us to pay our bills, work allows us to connect with our Creator and our communities. It gives us viable forums to share our unique gifts and talents in association with others. Work is not just a means of providing only for our needs and those of our families. Work also makes resources available to others in our communities, in our nation, and around the globe.

Listen to the Divine Voice Within You

It has become so common to pay attention to the many outer voices of the world that many of us are having difficulty recognizing the Divine voice within. Yet, our inner voice is probably the most direct and personal communication we will ever get from God. And only we can discern how to share our unique desires or dreams in accordance with that voice.

Discerning our God-given desires can be difficult. It requires a lot of careful thought. For some it may mean striking out on their own in pursuit of their passions, taking the road less traveled without a well-defined map. For others it may require making numerous career or geographic changes as they each discover their way. For a great number of us, however, it means doing exactly what we have been doing, but with a renewed sense of purpose—to share the joy, wisdom, and knowledge that is inside of us. And for everyone it means giving love, the most precious gift entrusted to us.

Be Used Up—*Not Burned Out*

Many of us feel so burned out these days that we have little left over to give others. The burnout generally is not from giving too much of ourselves—it's from not being in touch with our dreams and our higher purpose. We too often try to give from an empty place.

As George Bernard Shaw said, "This is the true joy in life...being used for a purpose recognized by yourself as a mighty one…being a force of nature instead of a feverish, selfish little clod of ailments and grievances complaining that the world will not devote itself to making you happy…. I am of the opinion that my life belongs to the whole community, and as long as I live it is my privilege to do for it whatever I can. I want to be thoroughly used up when I die. For the harder I work the more I live. I rejoice in life for its own sake. Life is no brief candle to me; it is a sort of splendid torch which I have got a hold of for the moment, and I want to make it burn as brightly as possible before handing it on to future generations."

As we prepare to pass the torch from our generation to the next, how many of us are living lives that belong to our communities? Will we be thoroughly used up when we die? Have too many of us let age become our excuse? Age was not an excuse for people like Senator Claude Pepper, Mahatma Gandhi, and Mother Teresa, who all began making their most significant contributions in the same age range as many of today's Retirees.

Consider the career of Albert Schweitzer. He began his adult years as a renowned musician. He then switched tracks and became an acclaimed theologian, philosopher, and writer. At 30, he attended medical school, and by 38 he established a hospital in West Africa, taking care of the needy. After World War I, he discovered that his hospital was in ruins and all that he had worked for had collapsed.

At nearly 50, however, Schweitzer rebuilt the hospital and ran it until his death at 90. He drew his life's energy from selfless giving. As Schweitzer wrote: "You must give some time to your fellow man. Even if it is a little thing, do something for those who have a need of help, something for which you can get no pay but the privilege of doing it. For remember, you don't live in a world all of your own. Your brothers are here too."

Have you withdrawn from being an active participant in making a meaningful difference in life? A man quoted in Dr. Stephen Covey's *First Things First* answers the question this way: "As I began to think about what matters the most to me, I suddenly realized that over the past years, that feeling, that sense of purpose, has somehow gotten lost. I've been lulled by a sense of security. I haven't made a difference. I've basically been watching life go by through the hedges of my country club."

Don't Take Your God-Given Dreams to the Grave

Like any muscle in life, at any age, if it is not exercised regularly it begins to waste away. Similarly, if dreams and desires are not generously shared and used, their effectiveness for giving life and co-creating will inevitably degenerate. Unfortunately, we often take to our graves a host of dreams and desires that were like fine china displayed in the cabinet and hardly ever used.

Whether the cultivation of your dreams allows you to experience success in comparison with what others achieve during their lifetimes does not really matter in the end. What matters is that we use our God-given desires and abilities with love—in a way that allows each of us to better realize the potential of what the Creator designed us to become. What we are is a gift from God, and what we become is our gift back to Him.

At times this may mean stretching ourselves to pursue a big goal or ambition that, out of fear, we might have been avoiding. Doubt often holds us back. It's all too easy to fearfully say to ourselves: "Who are you to do something so grand? You're just an ordinary person!"

But ordinary people, every day, in every walk of life, are able to accomplish extraordinary things by trusting in a power greater than themselves. As Dr. Robert H. Schuller, bestselling author and founder of The Crystal Cathedral Ministries says, "Make your goals big enough for God to fit into them." If you think you can accomplish your dream without God's help, you need to have a bigger dream.

The only thing better than living the Dream is sharing it and helping others achieve it. The more we achieve the more we need to share. As it says in Luke 12:48, "To whom much is given, much is required." And no matter how big or small the deed may be, we need to do it with love. As Mother Teresa said, "It is not how much we do, but how much love we put in the doing. It is not how much we give, but how much love we put in the giving."

In the end, God doesn't measure how much we did in comparison to what others have done or for how long. The foolish pride within us does that. As long as we each look for frequent opportunities to share the Dream with others and co-create in worthwhile matters, we will have lived lives deserving of the words, "Well done, my good and faithful servant!"

"*Pride gets no pleasure out of having something, only having more of it than the next man. It is the comparison that makes you proud; the pleasure of being above the rest. It is a spiritual cancer: it eats up the very possibility of love, or contentment, or even common sense. God is trying to make us humble in order to make this moment possible.*"

—C.S. Lewis

Chapter 17

Pride, Not Money, Is the Root of Our Evils

*"The need to compare and evaluate one's standing is at
the center of our pride. It is our ego's most treasured resource."*
—Charlie Douglas—

During the bull market of the 1990s, as mentioned earlier, *Newsweek* ran a story, "The Whine of '99, Everyone Is Getting Rich, But Me." It related the sentiments of a 31-year-old electrical engineer at General Motors earning $60,000 a year. He said, "If I didn't know any better, I'd be perfectly happy with what I am doing. But it gets to me to see my peers, people I relate to, people my own age, doing better than I am. You start to feel discontent." He was not alone. Many of us were envious of those investors who appeared to be getting rich from the venture capital boom of the Internet.

The pursuit of money, as an end in itself, can become an addiction. Many people believe the amount of money they have makes a statement about themselves—the more they have the better they are, and the less they possess the more inferior they must be. Many of us have *so much* in comparison with the rest of the world, yet we may act, at times, as if life and God have conspired against us.

Most of us get more upset at the thought of the relatively few materially wealthy in our society than by the millions of poor in the world. It is all too easy to overlook the fact that nearly 33 million people in America face hunger, while worldwide close to 800 million live in absolute poverty.

The majority of Americans say they have no chance whatsoever of becoming financially rich in their current jobs, even though they feel more social pressure to buy bigger houses and fancier cars to keep up with their neighbors. We are continually reminded to be discontented with what we have, as the typical U.S. consumer is bombarded by thousands of advertisements daily. Will Rogers spoke wisely when he said, "Too many of us spend money we don't even have, to buy things we don't even need, to impress people we don't even like."

Your Self-Worth Is Far Greater Than Your Net Worth

In our society many people perceive that our self-worth is heavily determined by our net worth. But our self-worth is far more important than our net worth. No matter how we stack up financially, we tend to overvalue what others appear to have and undervalue what we really are.

It is common to fall into the "comparison trap" of comparing ourselves and our possessions to others and what they seem to possess. If we seem to have more than our peers, we feel superior—we believe we are ahead in the game of life. If they appear to have more than we do, we are often envious of them as we believe we are behind.

God has given us the gift of life for us to love others, but in many cases we have used our precious energy to compare ourselves with others and envy those we should love. Yet, the only comparison we need to engage in is how much has our love for God and others grown over time? Have we become more loving over the years?

High school and other class reunions help illustrate our need for exterior comparison. Rather than looking forward to seeing some familiar faces and reminiscing about the good old days, attendees often become anxious about how they look, and about the status of their relationships and careers.

The need to compare and evaluate one's standing is at the center of our pride. It is our ego's most treasured resource. As C.S. Lewis said of pride: "It gets no pleasure out of having something, only having more of it than the next man. It is the comparison that makes you proud; the pleasure of being above the rest. It is a spiritual cancer: it eats up the very possibility of love, or contentment, or even common sense."

Our inevitable comparison to others would be much healthier if we looked to the rest of the world instead of only to our little Western corner of it. The truth is that most of us have hit the jackpot without ever knowing it. There is a one in fifty chance of being born in America. And if one could shrink the Earth's population to a small village with all existing human ratios remaining the same, it would reveal the following: the majority of the villagers would live in substandard housing; most would be unable to read; many would suffer from malnutrition; and hardly anyone would have a college education or a computer.

Despite our relative economic good fortune, there is still a lot of restlessness in America today. Many expect the journey to begin with the end in sight. Often we fail to notice that much of the journey is beyond our control. And what is really needed for a successful trip is profound gratitude to God for the many blessings we have received. Yes, we need to set goals and diligently pursue them, but it's wise not to become attached to them. We can control a lot of the input but not the ultimate result.

Pray like it depends on God, and work like it depends on you. Give it everything you have, but don't be devastated if you don't get exactly what you thought you wanted. Trust that God can see in ways that we cannot.

Pride often thwarts our attempts to acquire financial capital too. It makes individual investors think they can handpick the hottest stocks and mutual funds. Yet these decisions are often ill-informed and ill-timed. They are usually based on past performance and information.

It is our prideful egos that can cause us to hold onto losing stocks far too long because we don't want to admit that we have made mistakes. Prideful thinking prevents us from investing in accordance with the discipline of asset allocation, and it leads us to believe we are smarter than the market. Most investors who proceed down pride's investment path come up well short of the market's general performance.

We need to be careful not to blame money, or the lack thereof, for many of our difficulties. Money, in and of itself, cannot be the root of any evil. Money always has been, is, and will remain an inanimate, neutral object. It is nothing more than a store of value and a medium of exchange. In reality, money and possessions by themselves offer very little, although Western culture appears to indicate otherwise. It is simply our attitudes toward them that determine how they affect us.

Imagine you could live anywhere in the world and have anything you wanted except love and people with whom to share it. How many of us would honestly choose that situation? The thought of being like Macaulay Culkin's character in *Home Alone,* with all the toys to ourselves, may appear to be enticing at first glance. But on further reflection, the things of this world have little to offer us in terms of lasting wealth.

Some argue that money is the root of all evil. They naively believe that the *Bible* supports their claim. The New Testament, however, reveals: "The love of money is a root of evil; and to let our lives be free from the love of money and to be content with what you have." Further, we are instructed to remember that: "…it is the *covetous* man who is never satisfied with money and the *lover* of wealth who reaps no fruit from it."

We have been endeavoring to get a handle on pride, some of us more successfully than others, ever since Adam and Eve. Why did Adam and Eve partake of the forbidden fruit? They ate the fruit because they naively believed they would become god-like. They were told by the serpent that the moment they ate the fruit they would be like gods who know what is good and what is evil. Mankind's first sin was one of pride, and today pride is still leading us astray.

Be Careful—*Your Thoughts Are Spiritual Currency*

Sigmund Freud believed that our behavior is best explained by the way we handle our basic instincts and thoughts regarding sex and aggression. To Freud, all of us want to be the king of the hill where we kill off the competition and have intimate relations with everyone whom we desire. If Freud is right, we may not be able to control a lot of what pops into our heads, or the goodness of our thoughts. But we do have something to say about the amount of time we spend entertaining less than worthwhile ambitions.

Even so, many times do we answer the knock on the door of our imaginations to find greed or envy outside, and we willingly welcome them in? Too often, we mentally entertain these prideful "intruders" long after they should have worn out their welcome. The more time they are given, however, the more likely they are to obtain our souls' consent.

Often, we flirt with danger by allowing unwholesome thoughts to become habitual. And sooner or later, "innocent" thoughts that have long been entertained find their way into our actions. In fact, most actions are born out of a prior thought. Therefore, in a sense, our thoughts are a type of spiritual currency.

As in the "Parable of the Sower," we hear the call to love God and others, but then worldly anxiety and the lure of riches may choke our efforts, allowing them to bear little fruit. Pride often gets the best of us when we forget we are here to love and make a difference in the world—not just to compete for secular glory. When we reject our duty to love, we lose our way.

Be Humble—*Ignore Pride*

The cure for pride is humility. Selflessness eradicates unhealthy competition because our focus shifts to a purpose greater than ourselves and our own desires. Where there is true humility there is no need to judge and compare. Humble people understand that the world is bigger than they are individually, and that they were never meant to be on center stage for very long.

Perhaps having humility is best viewed as envisioning God as a loving artist, painting a portrait of our lives as part of the mural of creation. In one sense, we are a little paintbrush and need to trust that the Artist alone has the skill for realizing every precise detail. But at the same time, we need to use our God-given abilities and desires. This helps to bring out the defining lines of meaningful character through right thought and action.

Being humble does not mean thinking of ourselves as deficient and lowly. It is not found in the belittling of oneself but foremost in ignoring one's ego. It does not require a poor self-image or lack of self-respect. On the contrary, as Nelson Mandela stated, "Our deepest fear is not that we are inadequate.... It is our light, not our darkness, that most frightens us. We ask ourselves, who am I to be brilliant, gorgeous, talented, and fabulous? Actually, who are you not to be?" When we get past our narcissistic self—our self-centered nature—our true radiance shines. After all, we are the most brilliant color seen in all creation.

Add Prayer First—*and You'll Start to Find Humility*
Humility is best acquired by a gradual change in one's heart that often begins with faithful prayer. Still, many of us seek God through prayer only when we experience sickness, loss, and other difficulties.

Somehow it is all too easy to feel that God is distant or inattentive to our daily concerns. But could it be that we are the ones who are not paying attention to God? Perhaps we don't receive grace because we may not realize we need it, or we have not sought it with firm faith. Prayer brings God into our lives, not necessarily according to our desires, but according to God's loving will.

As Mother Teresa said, "I do not think there is anyone who needs God's help and grace as much as I do. Sometimes I feel so helpless and weak. Because I cannot depend upon my own strength, I rely on Him 24 hours a day." Mother Teresa's secret was very simple: she prayed constantly, and believed that all of us need to cling to God through prayer.

It is of little importance how each of us prays in accordance with our particular faith. What is significant, however, is to pursue God every day through faithful prayer. Real prayer is more than what we say to God. Perhaps the greatest blessing of prayer is that we stay still long enough to hear what God may have to say to us.

Faithful prayer will help change you or your circumstances, and it often doesn't matter which happens first. It is our most sincere way of asking for the wisdom of God's love to guide our lives. When we feel lonely, unworthy, sick, and forgotten, we are still precious to God. The act of praying combats the pride of trusting in only ourselves. Prayer keeps us connected to the source of all love. As Rev. Paul Deever says, "Prayer is the Internet of the soul, reaching around the world."

With each new day, God gives us a gift of another 86,400 seconds. Surely we can use a few of them to reconnect with our Creator. But prayer alone is not enough to do away with pride. That requires actively caring for others.

"The deepest need of man is the need to overcome his separateness, to leave the prison of his aloneness. We need to experience spiritual and emotional union. Only through loving and giving can we leave the prison cells of our aloneness. We must make someone else's needs as important as our own."

—Eric Fromm

Chapter 18

Serving Others—The Surest Way to Let Go and Let God

*"For many of us it may be that our faith alone in God
assures salvation—but it is our works on behalf of others that most
assuredly provide the best evidence of our faith."*
—Charlie Douglas—

W hen feeling worried or overwhelmed, most of us, at some point, with various degrees of success, have tried to let go of our concerns and give them to God. As many of us have experienced, the notion of "letting go and letting God" is easier said than done. Why? The ego likes to maintain control.

The Ego's Grasp on the Nets We Carry

When we are truly able to quiet the ego and trust in a higher power, there is often an undeniable sense of relief. It is as if a burdensome weight has been lifted from our shoulders. God, however, doesn't necessarily take away our concerns simply as a result of our prayers and earnest desire on our part to let go. Something more is frequently required. Many times, we need to loosen the grip on our own concerns and selflessly stretch out our hands in service to others.

The movie titled *The Mission* helps illustrates this point. In the beginning scenes, a ruthless captain tracks down island natives to be used as slave labor for a king. After one such successful conquest, the captain returns to town and discovers his girlfriend in bed with his brother. Blinded by pride and anger, the captain kills his brother. Thereafter, the captain is overcome by intense feelings of guilt and remorse. He suffers great emotional agony and a missionary priest tries to help the broken captain in his anguish. The priest asks the captain to fulfill a painstakingly difficult penance to cleanse him of his sin and release him from his torment.

His penance is to follow a group of missionaries up a steep waterfall, while carrying his cumbersome weapons and armor in a net behind him—the outward evidence of all that he has become. The assent is extremely strenuous and the captain falls hard many times in the process, but he is unwilling to accept any assistance from others. During the climb, a missionary priest in the group pleads for the captain's penance to come to an end, convinced that he has suffered long enough. Yet the priest who issued the penance disagrees and tells his contemporary, "The captain doesn't feel it is yet time. Only he will know when his penance is done, when it is time to finally let go."

As the missionaries reach a crest, they encounter several natives from a tribe that the captain had formerly hunted down. Bloodied and near collapse, the captain finally reaches the group and is immediately face to face with a native who has drawn his knife. But instead of wielding the knife upon the captain in revenge, the native mercifully cuts the captain's weighty net. It is only then that the captain is released from his tremendous burden, his penance finally completed. Thereafter, the captain commits his life to God and spends the rest of his days in service to the mission and the natives who live there.

The captain was finally free of his torment but, in a sense, the priest who issued the penance had been wrong. It's not that the penance issued was wrong, but that the captain alone did not know when his penance was done, when it was time for him to let go. Without the native's merciful act of love, the prideful captain would have continued to carry his heavy burden until he collapsed. Many of us are like the captain. We fail to realize that it often takes God and acts of service, both to and from others, to truly let go.

Letting Go Takes More Than One Step

In everyday life, letting go is perhaps best illustrated by the millions of alcoholics who have found solace through the distinguished 12-step program of Alcoholics Anonymous. In the book *Alcoholics Anonymous,* the essence of many alcoholics' undoing is revealed: "Selfishness and self-centeredness! That, we think, is the root of our troubles. What usually happens in the alcoholic's life is that the show doesn't come off very well. He becomes, on the next occasion, still more demanding or gracious, as the case may be. Still the play doesn't suit him. Admitting he may be somewhat at fault, he is sure that other people are more to blame. He becomes angry, indignant, and self-pitying. Therefore, and above everything else, we alcoholics must be free of this selfishness. We must or it kills us!"

Many of the alcoholics who gave their personal testimonies in that book possessed exceptional credentials. Curiously, not one of them was able to break his or her addiction through using willpower. Instead, all turned to a higher power for help in overcoming the addiction. But if admitting you are an alcoholic, powerless, and willing to surrender your life to a higher power were enough to cure you of your dependency on alcohol, there would be only three steps to the program, not twelve.

The alcoholic also needs to take a fearless moral inventory, make a list of those whom he or she has harmed, and make amends to such people wherever possible. In addition, a recovering alcoholic needs to carry the message of his or her spiritual awakening and service to other alcoholics.

In short, alcoholics rid themselves of pride and selfishness, not only by their trust in a higher power, but also through service to others. Although most of us do not have to endure a debilitating addiction like alcoholism, all of us can identify with our own areas of self-centeredness.

To help us cope with our difficulties today, antidepressants and professional counselors are in great demand. The number of Americans treated for depression nearly tripled in the 1990s. And while confiding in a trained therapist may also be helpful, the potential drawback of most therapy is that the spotlight remains brightly fixed on the patient. People can spend years and vast amounts of money in therapy dealing with the same issues, yet never really get beyond themselves.

Much like when we focus on the throb of a toothache, continual self-examination of our difficulties may only serve to intensify the pain. While there is a time and place for professional counseling, many of us might be healthier emotionally if we worked through our difficulties, while lovingly turning our attention toward helping others. This can cause an amazing catharsis and healing.

There are countless ways to serve the needs of others. Institutionally, there are over one million nonprofit entities. While nearly 100-million volunteers are assisting them in some way, they can always use more help. Less formally, there are also plenty of opportunities presented to us daily to be kind and caring to others.

How to Amass Spiritual Capital

The ways to fashion spiritual capital will be limited only by our failure to think creatively. Consider the following short list as a starter on how to amass spiritual capital:

- If appropriate, buy a meal for and spend some time with a homeless person, or at least send that person your silent blessing when your paths cross.
- Volunteer to do someone else's chores around the house even though it is really that person's turn.
- Make it a priority to pay three people a sincere compliment before the day ends.
- Take the money that you were going to spend at "happy hour" and start a charitable "piggy bank" with your kids.
- Take a few kids on the little league team out for ice cream when they lose, if they have played hard and had fun, because it is just a game.
- Pay the bill at the drive-through window or a highway toll for the person behind you.
- Before having dinner tonight pray with your family and share one thing that each of you was grateful for during the day.
- Forward a personal note of congratulations to someone who has had a recent success.

- Spend ten minutes alone in nature with the Creator, giving thanks for all that you have.

We need to do our best to give, at least in some small way, to all those whom we meet every day. It may be as simple as smiling and saying hello, or being a good listener. When we seek to sincerely acknowledge and understand those around us, however, we cannot fail to love them.

Pay It Forward—*Pass on to Three Others the Good Deed That Was Done for You*

A few years ago there was a movie titled *Pay It Forward*. It provided a compelling look at a model for producing spiritual capital. The general theme was that our world would be a much better place if each of us did a good deed for three other people. The movie inspired us to pass on to others the good deed that was done for us without expectations and for no particular reason other than to be kind. Upon receiving the favors, these three people would then be asked, in turn, to "pay it forward" to another three people, thereby creating an exponential growth of spiritual capital.

During the Kosovo crisis at the end of the 1990s, I became aware of a good example of paying it forward. Some friends in Los Angeles had learned from a server at dinner one evening of a local refugee family in need. For several months, they generously welcomed that immigrant family as part of their own. They began by buying a few simple things for the family like food and clothes.

As they opened themselves up more to the many possibilities of giving, however, they also provided costly dental care for the family members. They even looked for ways to make it possible for the family to have a place of its own. My friends could not take a charitable tax deduction for the time and money they had spent in assisting the refugees, but their unselfish acts of love were their own reward.

Adding to the societal treasury of spiritual capital doesn't have to be as elaborate and involved as helping a refugee family. It can be as simple as giving a smile to those who cross our paths every day. Recently, I read a sign at a car rental agency counter which extolled the value of a smile. It read something like this:

> SMILE! It costs nothing to give, but creates much. It not only enriches those who receive it, but also those who give it. None of us are so rich that we can get along without it. It creates happiness in a home and fosters goodwill in a business. And it is something that is no good until it is given away.

Some altruistic acts, even one simple deed, can benefit the integrity of an institution. Baseball, America's favorite pastime, received a much-needed shot in the arm when a young man named Tim Forneris scooped up Mark McGwire's illustrious 62nd home-run ball—the hit that broke Roger Marris's long-standing record.

Before the homerun was hit, prognosticators everywhere talked about how much the prized ball would bring to the lucky person who retrieved it. It was also rumored that the IRS would assess a gift tax on the transfer of the ball if it were sold for less than its fair market value.

But all pundits were fittingly silenced when the young St. Louis groundskeeper simply returned the ball so it could be given back to McGwire, saying, "It's not mine to begin with. McGwire just lost it, and I brought it home. I'm a regular Joe."

Two seasons later, that selfless example of the young groundskeeper was completely ignored by two grown men. They fought like little kids for well over a year-and-a-half regarding Barry Bonds' record-setting-73rd-homerun ball. Like a must-have toy that two siblings fuss over, that ball brought nothing but disagreement. In the end, the judge ruled that the prized ball be sold and the proceeds be evenly split. Yet, the ball commanded an auction price of only $450,000, whereas McGwire's 70th-homerun ball of

1999 sold for $3.2 million. Fittingly, the $450,000 may not have been enough to cover even the legal fees of the lawyers that each man had employed!

Perhaps the biggest opportunity for service in our materialistic culture is to help meet a person's intangible needs as opposed to his or her tangible ones. Often people are lonely even though they have many material comforts. Spiritual poverty is, in fact, worse than financial poverty. Eric Fromm, psychoanalyst and best-selling author of *The Art of Loving,* put it this way: "The deepest need of man is the need to overcome his separateness, to leave the prison of his aloneness. We need to experience spiritual and emotional union. Only through loving and giving can we leave the prison cells of our aloneness. We must make someone else's needs as important as our own."

The Highest Worship of God Is Found in Serving Mankind

For many of us it may be that our faith alone in God assures salvation—but it is our works on behalf of others that most assuredly provide the best evidence of our faith. I believe very strongly in the words of St. Francis, "Preach the Gospel at all times [through your actions]; when necessary, use words."

At the end of our lives we will not be judged by how many degrees we have, how much money we've made, or how far up the world's ladder we have climbed. If there is any judgment by our Creator, it will be: "I was hungry and you gave me food; I was thirsty and you gave me drink; a stranger and you welcomed me; naked and you clothed me; ill and you cared for me; in prison and you visited me."

We are told that we will always have the poor with us, but that doesn't mean we are not supposed to help them change their situations. Care for the poor will no doubt require our time, training, and monetary assistance. But the poor must not be seen as a burden—they are our brothers and sisters too. They represent an opportunity to experience the love of God by practicing the virtue of kindness.

We need to encourage the poor to reconnect with society and become productive participants. Government can help economically distressed areas by granting special incentives for businesses to expand there. These tax incentives, known as Enterprise Zones, provide stimulus to create new jobs and investments that benefit the poor who are living in designated areas. But governmental assistance alone is not the entire solution.

The poor not only lack material goods; they often lack the knowledge and skills to change their circumstances. The principle of solidarity, therefore, is best lived out by helping the poor find the hope they so desperately need.

Habitat for Humanity, a nonprofit, ecumenical Christian housing ministry, provides an excellent example of helping people get back on their feet, while still asking them to walk under their own power. Through volunteer labor and donations, Habitat provides proper housing to partner families at no profit. Such housing is financed with no-interest loans. Partner families, however, do not get a free handout. They must provide the down payment and make the monthly mortgage payments. Additionally, they must also invest hundreds of hours of their own labor—sweat equity—into building their Habitat house and the houses of others.

As of today, Habitat has built more than 150,000 houses around the world, providing appropriate housing for over 700,000 people in more than 3,000 communities. Former U.S. President and Nobel Peace Prize winner Jimmy Carter and his wife, Rosalynn, have been crusaders for Habitat since 1984, bringing global publicity to Habitat. Yet, Habitat's ministry remains a simple one: Christ's love must not be expressed in words alone. It must be true love, which shows itself in action as the "theology of the hammer."

We Are Called to Be God's Visible Hands

Our faith and our concept of religion must not become just a club that we join merely as card-carrying members who believe God is supposed to make us successful. As mentioned earlier, there may well be an "invisible hand," which, as set forth by Adam Smith, guides our actions toward increasing our societal wealth, even though we are simply pursuing economic self-interest. That, however, does not mean God is conducting unseen capitalistic works. Instead, we are called to be God's "visible hands," working in a free enterprise system.

We need to help proclaim that human life is sacred and that the dignity of each person is the foundation of our society and our institutions. People are more important than things, and our institutions need to become more effective at improving life and promoting the dignity of everyone. They need to reflect concern for others and help bring about social justice.

Our care and use of the environment and its resources need to become more than Earth Day annual remembrances. The challenge for us is to live every day believing that we are one human family, regardless of our national, ethnic, economic, religious, ideological, and other differences. In doing so, "loving our neighbor" will have global implications as economies everywhere serve the people, not the other way around.

Give Until It Hurts—*Not Just Until It Feels Good*

Philanthropist Claude Rosenberg, the author of *Wealthy and Wise,* and past chairman of an investment company worth $60 billion, spent many years researching and analyzing America's giving abilities and habits. Most of us find it easier to give only until it feels good—not until it hurts. Rosenberg firmly believes by his estimates, that if we Americans were to make charitable donations closer to our comfortable capacities, even in bear markets, we could invest at least $100 billion dollars more each year in solving societal ills.

Consider the witty comments of Ted Turner when he graciously donated $1 billion to the United Nations: "My net worth on January 1, 1997, was $2.2 billion—on August 1, 1997, it was $3.2 billion. I'm only giving away nine months of income!" Although his contributions were significant, Turner, nonetheless, was not hampered financially by his decision to give. Most of us who give monetarily are just like Ted Turner, only there are fewer zeros behind the $1.

Maybe the most honest and selfish reason for giving is that we know there is an emotional emptiness deep inside of us that needs healing. We have a great need to be loved. So often today, natural feelings of such emptiness are quickly masked over with food, television, and other things belonging to the material world. But allowing ourselves to fully feel these voids can present opportunities for holiness and the growth of our spiritual capital.

Consider that physical hunger through fasting is sought after precisely because it puts us in the position to purify our souls. Every major world religion today promotes fasting because it allows one to discover self-control over the body and its appetites. It also enables us to experience compassion for those who are physically impoverished.

Learn From Both a Princess and a Pauper

I found it more than a mere coincidence that Mother Teresa and Princess Diana died within five days of one another. The two were friends and perhaps even kindred spirits. But Princess Diana was more like the adolescent student struggling to find love, while Mother Teresa resembled the seasoned teacher who wrote the book on it.

In many ways, Princess Diana lived the fairy-tale life that many of us desire. When Diana became a princess, she was instantly showered with money, elaborate clothes and jewels, celebrity status, and millions of admirers. But as we got to know a little more about the real Diana, we learned that she was desperate to find love.

Money, a mind-boggling wardrobe, and the most photographed face in the world did not provide her with the love for which she yearned. And although Diana experienced love through her children and a few close family members and friends, it was in her moments of selfless public service to the less fortunate that Diana experienced love in the most special way. In particular, she graciously focused the media's attention on worthy causes for humanity, like the elimination of land mines.

After Diana's tragic death, she was honored with a memorial service that was second to none. It included tons of flowers, millions of mourners who watched from around the world, and a song that was written and sung in tribute to her by Elton John. When the Arts and Entertainment Television Network (A&E) did a special on the 100 most significant people over the past 1,000 years, they named her number 73. Maybe Diana was so extraordinarily special because she was not only a princess but, in many ways, she was like us.

When her friend Mother Teresa died five days later, the Associated Press first advised us of her death, with the headline: "Mother Teresa Dead." They expanded the headline the next day: "Mother Teresa—the tiny saint of the gutters whose untiring ministry to the poor and terminally ill made her synonymous with charity—died yesterday of a massive heart attack."

The local paper in Calcutta carried a cartoon depicting a mosque, a Hindu temple, a Buddhist temple, and a Christian church. Outside each building, members representing these religions stood dressed in their respective religious attire with their hands joined together in prayer as they looked up to heaven. The caption underneath it simply read: "O God, please do not take our Mother away from us."

The memorial service for Mother Teresa was well-attended, but it did not outwardly compare to the one held for Princess Diana. The Nobel Peace Prize-winning nun didn't even make A&E's list! But something tells me that's just the way Mother Teresa would have wanted it. After all, she owned nothing except three sets of habits made of coarse cloth.

Yet Mother Teresa lived a life rich with love because she had many years of bringing joy to the faces of abandoned babies, seeing smiles light up the faces of disabled children, helping the dying poor go home to God in peace, holding the hands of AIDS patients, restoring dignity to leprosy sufferers, and bringing the healing touch of God's love to the sick and lonely.

Mother Teresa believed that God used her to accomplish great things because she believed more in her Creator's love than in her own human abilities. Her love for Jesus was not based on what He could give to her. She selflessly loved Him through her calling because that is what He asked of her. Selfless acts of service, whether done by a princess or a pauper, are the surest ways to let go of self-centeredness and bring more love into the world.

" **A**nd for the support of this declaration, with a firm reliance on the protection of Divine Providence, we mutually pledge to each other our lives, our fortunes, and our sacred honor."

—The Declaration of Independence

Chapter 19

Awakening the American Dream Bringing Spiritual and Financial Capital Together

"The American Dream, grounded in love, is not America's message to the world; it is our Creator's message to humanity."
—Charlie Douglas—

In its relatively short history, America has experienced several periods of renewal and spiritual reform. They were times of revitalization—a reorientation in beliefs and values toward our founding principles, encouraging faith and civic virtue. These periods, known as awakenings, brought God and our nation closer together.

The Great Awakening of religious devoutness swept through the American colonies between the 1730s and 1770s. A second awakening took place during the period of moral decline after the Revolutionary War. Awakenings also occurred during the industrialization and urbanization of America at the beginning of the twentieth century, and again as the Roaring 20s ended, leading into the Great Depression.

As we go forward in the twenty-first century, we are being summoned, once again, to draw from that principled well of our Founding Fathers.

Since the beginning of humanity, God and the material world have seemingly coaxed us in differing directions with the message, "Come follow me."

It would be wonderful to set forth a simple *how-to formula* that would allow us to uniformly claim the wages of both our

Creator and the material world. But that is not the way of life. By their intrinsic nature, there will always be some opposing tensions in the pursuit of God's Kingdom and a materially based American Dream. We each have a body and a soul, which, for the time being, link us with both the material and spiritual worlds.

God is the loving force emanating from the world of spirit found in our hearts and souls. The pursuit of money as an end in and of itself, on the other hand, tends to keep us bound to the material world. Jesus' admonition in Matthew 6:24 and Luke 16:13 regarding the inability to serve two masters simultaneously, makes it clear that tough choices often need to be made. Be that as it may, serving God, being a good steward, and increasing our standard of living can all be components in living out the American Dream.

We Need to Change Our Thinking—*in Order to Create Lasting Wealth*

Our quest to bring financial and spiritual capital together in the pursuit of the American Dream is challenging, but these two elements can be made to work together for good. A lot depends on our attitude and discernment.

While most of us clearly understand what is meant by financial capital, spiritual capital can be more difficult to grasp. In summary, spiritual capital is nothing more than those intangible assets that result from responsibly using our God-given gifts, talents, and dreams in a fruitful fashion. Anytime we are doing unto others as we would like others to do unto us, loving our neighbors as ourselves, or co-creating in a worthwhile manner, we are adding to society's treasury of spiritual capital. If we want our lives to be masterpieces and we desire to create lasting wealth, we need to change our thinking about the so-called incompatibilities of these two essential capitals.

Throughout the course of history, some religious truths that were initially thought to be incongruent with other approaches to understanding life are now viewed as congruent—someone had the courage to color outside the lines. For example, many once thought that human intelligence and the ability to reason were irreconcilable with God and Divine revelation—until St. Thomas Aquinas took the logic of Aristotle and applied it to faith.

Aquinas used his inspired intellect to see beyond the widely held traditional religious beliefs of his day. He taught that reason was supportive of revelation and that our common sense was an important part in defining religious virtues. During his time, Aquinas's teachings were undeniably radical, and some viewed him as a heretic. Today, ironically, St. Thomas Aquinas is the favored theologian of many Christian conservatives.

Similarly, science and psychology were once thought to be incompatible with religion. For example, Galileo's belief that the Earth revolved around the sun (and not vice versa) was once preached as being in direct conflict with Christian theology. Yet, today, we understand this to be true and wholly consistent.

In fact, science, religion, and psychology are now viewed as three disciplines that provide meaningful approaches to help us deal effectively with the human condition. Today, these three disciplines are generally seen holistically and mutually cooperative with one another, although one may be more appropriate than another in dealing with a specific situation. For instance, if our daughter (or son) is suffering from an infection, we may pray for her health, hold her hand, and talk to her to bring her emotional comfort; but we generally depend most upon an antibiotic to cure the infection.

The pursuit of financial and spiritual capital, both of which are inherent in the American Dream, has areas of genuine compatibility. We just need to look past their apparent dissimilarities. The noble pursuit of capitalism through self-interest often yields more than unintended acts of service. In many cases, a free market system inspires many intended acts of beneficial service. Receiving money as a result of extending caring service to others advances the Kingdom of God. So, too, does using money to improve the quality of life and to foster human dignity.

There is no magic recipe regarding lasting wealth, such as "x" part financial capital and "y" part spiritual capital. We need both spiritual and financial capital in varying amounts for our personal well-being and our society's welfare. As Pope John Paul II stated, "...the person and society need not only material goods but spiritual and religious values as well."

Wisely Choose Life's "BIG Things"

The American Dream is best nurtured and kept alive when we are true to ourselves, and are willing to explore our personal histories. Socrates, who was dedicated to understanding and achieving virtue, said, "The unexamined life isn't worth living." With this in mind, creating lasting wealth requires some soul-searching and self-examination. In that regard, each has a personal destiny worth uncovering and passing on.

A good example of this is found in the book *Tuesdays with Morrie,* written by Mitch Albom. In this true-life story, a former student is reunited with his mentor, a college professor named Morrie, who is dying. In the last months of Morrie's life, the two get together every Tuesday as Morrie openly shares his wisdom about life and prepares to accept death.

In one of his lessons Morrie candidly talks about the need for us to develop our own subculture. He states: "I don't mean you disregard every rule of your community. I don't go around naked, for example. I don't go through red lights. The little things I can obey. But the big things—how we think, what we value—those you must choose for yourself. You can't let anyone—or any society—determine those for you."

A skilled facilitator can help evaluate the merits of your personal history and provide assistance in uncovering your personal destiny. Ultimately, however, it is up to you to determine what is worth building with your life's energy, and what kind of legacy you intend to leave behind. You must choose these things in accordance with your own conscience. But wise choices always stem from an informed conscience. And the key to making wise decisions is that they be based on the notion of virtues—strength of character applied to daily living.

As we clarify our own core values, we need to do so within the context of non-economic assets that can lead to virtues. To become virtuous requires that we practice discernment based on our life experiences and careful reflection. This is how we put ourselves in the position to temper our self-interest.

The virtue of lasting wealth is found in wisely and freely choosing your direction in life. Abiding by laws and imposed rules alone doesn't make us virtuous. We're just complying with what other people have established for us. Virtue, on the other hand, is about developing wisdom, over time, gained through living life. It is about living with compassion and respect for human dignity.

Pope John Paul II said in his *Encyclical Letter, Evangelium Vitae 71*—"It is urgently necessary, for the future of society and the development of a sound democracy, to rediscover those essential and innate human and moral values which flow from the very truth of the human being and express and safeguard the dignity of the human person: values which no individual, no majority and no State can ever create, modify or destroy, but must only acknowledge, respect and promote."

Human freedom and liberty are necessary prerequisites to forming virtue in our lives. Otherwise, we would be like all other animals that are ruled by their instincts or the dictates of their masters. What distinguishes us from animals is our *intelligence,* which can recognize various degrees of good and evil, and our *will,* which chooses from among them. Human freedom has been granted to us so we can support each other in love. In doing so, we need to choose wisely among those commitments which are based on love.

For wealth to endure, it, like a seed, needs fertile soil in which it can thrive. Spiritual capital is like the unseen roots of a flower that keep it grounded and nourished. Whereas, financial capital is often like a blooming flower that can be garnered and admired. It is the beauty of the bloom, in particular, that attracts the eye and tugs at our egos. Yet, if financial capital becomes our primary focus we tend to neglect the roots, which, over time, causes the flower to wither and die. Without the context of values and the non-economic assets that are found in the process of building spiritual capital, financial capital loses much of its potency.

A short-sighted view in business, for example, may focus principally on gathering the financial bloom of sales, instead of creating a lasting relationship with budding service. It can be as simple as the difference between making a one-time sale to a new prospect, versus building a business of satisfied customers over the long-term.

Realize the American Dream by Helping Others Achieve *Their* Dreams

Almost everything we accomplish of importance in life we do with and through other people. Capitalism works only if people remain associative and continue to work to help one another. Therefore, an effective way for you to realize the American Dream is to help others accomplish their dreams too.

A friend of mine, Greg Reid, built a successful premium business selling simple products like pens and magnets. He developed his business, not by focusing on making money for himself; rather, he succeeded by concentrating on helping his employees become successful themselves. He mentored his employees to get what they desired by having them first provide enthusiastic service to customers. The goal in each case is to get what you want by first helping others to get what they want. Today, Greg invests his time mentoring others outside of the workplace and has written down his helping-others approach to success in a parable titled *The Millionaire Mentor.*

Helping others reach their dreams is a big part of capitalism. Network marketing companies and organizations, in particular, embrace this principle. Person-to-person marketing used to sound strange to many of us. The products once marketed were every-day consumer staples only.

Now it is a multi-billion-dollar industry, and anything imaginable can be purchased through these home-based business professionals located throughout the world. Built on the principle of helping others reach their dreams, network marketing entrepreneurs can earn spiritual and financial capital at the same time.

Beyond small business and network marketing, many large corporations built their businesses by creating win-win environments. In the book *Loyalty Rules!—How Today's Leaders Build Lasting Relations,* author Frederick F. Reichheld makes the point that companies such as Enterprise Rent-A-Car, Vanguard, Northwestern Mutual Insurance, Cisco, Intuit, Dell Computer, Southwest Airlines, and Harley-Davidson all became successful because they stressed building mutually beneficial relationships.

One standout company in particular, Chick-fil-A, deserves special recognition. Founded by S. Truett Cathy, this fast-food franchise, which sells chicken, was built around Cathy's leadership of putting the welfare of others first. By focusing on helping the people around him have better lives, Truett Cathy experienced tremendous success of his own.

He built his business based on biblical principles, and to this day, all the restaurants are closed on Sunday to "ensure every Chick-fil-A employee and restaurant owner has an opportunity to worship, spend time with family and friends, or just plain rest from the work week."

Its corporate purpose is: "To glorify God by being faithful stewards of all that is entrusted to us. To have a positive influence on all who come in contact with Chick-fil-A." Integrating biblical principles with good business practices has yielded some rather impressive results. Today, Chick-fil-A has more than 1,000 restaurants nationwide, with over $1.25 billion in combined sales.

Use the 80/20 Rule for Nontraditional Planning

People don't normally fail in their plans regarding wealth so much as they fail to understand the true meaning of wealth. Most people spend 80 percent of their time focusing on traditional wealth planning, usually soliciting the advice of financial planners, estate planners, tax accountants, and insurance agents. The goal is often to obtain a traditional deliverable (investment model, trust, tax return, and such) as quickly and as economically as possible.

The problem with this planning is that these hired agents generally make recommendations through the rose-colored glasses of the world they know. They generally add little value because only 20 percent of the time is spent on helping the clients get in touch with and implement their core values. Planning for lasting wealth, on the other hand, may require investing up to 80 percent of the time for establishing objectives, determining core values, and crafting family mission statements surrounding shared values, goals, and dreams. As little as 20 percent of the time can be spent focusing on procuring the traditional deliverables.

Years ago, the railroads failed to adapt to the changing needs of the marketplace because they saw themselves as being in the railroad business, rather than the transportation industry. Likewise, in my business today, I no longer believe that I am in the legal or financial profession in the traditional sense. My reason for being in business is to help others wisely accumulate and pass on lasting wealth through values-based and multi-generational planning.

In the spring of 2003, Boston College researchers Paul Schervish and John Havens released a report confirming the largest intergenerational wealth transfer in history. According to the report, *Why the $41 Trillion Wealth Transfer Is Still Valid—A Review of Challenges and Questions,* at least $41 trillion of assets will be transferred by 2052, with approximately $25 trillion going directly to heirs. With so much material wealth changing hands, people need proficient counsel to help them make wise financial choices in passing on a lasting wealth that promotes individual liberty as well as the common good.

Seek to Find God in All Things

Lasting wealth is also procured where God is sought in all things, regardless of what you do or your economic circumstances. No job, business, or financial asset has a higher or lower ranking in and of itself. We can approach each in a way where we are either going away from or toward God—it's always our choice. Each one of us is but a small part of creation orbiting around our Creator. The happiest and most successful people I know put God first, their families second, and their jobs or businesses third.

How can someone with a professional career and millions of dollars be unhappy and insecure? How could anyone who has experienced an abundance of material success, near the top of the ladder, not be filled with gratitude that he or she has received more than his or her share of blessings? And why is it that another who climbs the worldly ladder curses those at the top? It's simply because they are not seeking God in all things. As long as you have God in your heart, regardless of your financial position or your level of accomplishment, you will be joyful.

Finding God in all things comes through focusing on the inspired dreams that come from our Creator, working on becoming neutral to riches and poverty, and surrendering our attachments to outcomes. It means living in the present and doing our best to experience and express God's love in all that we think, say, and do. And although we need to graciously take things as they come, we still need to work hard to make things happen.

Fight to Keep the Dream Alive

Recently, I attended a function in Washington, D.C. where bestselling author William Bennett was one of the featured speakers. That night Bennett, in his typical fashion, delivered a skillful message of conviction regarding engaging in the "good fight" for fundamental principles.

For many in the audience, William Bennett represented the bold crusader. For years, he had capably made a clear case regarding the need for moral clarity in an often ambiguous world. The next day, however, the news media reported that Bennett had wagered millions in casinos during the past decade. Suddenly, all appeared not to be well in the land of virtue.

Bennett's enemies seized the moment to lash out. Michael Kinsley, columnist for *The Washington Post,* took great delight in writing, "Sinners have long cherished the fantasy that William Bennett, the virtue magnate, might be among our number."

Others came to Bennett's defense. Unexpectedly, Bennett's political adversary, Mario Cuomo, former governor of New York, quickly dismissed any taint of sin that may have been committed by Bennett saying, "Gambling is not a sin; it's not illegal. He [Bennett] didn't condemn it and then contradict himself. He didn't hurt anyone. He didn't lie about it; he didn't try to hide it." Gambling, according to Cuomo, is "not among the seven great sins or even among the 70 smaller ones."

In part, Cuomo is right. Gambling, in some places, certainly is allowed by civil law, and it is not directly contrary to Divine law.

However, because gambling can lead to excess and addiction, acts of gambling have been forbidden by both civil and religious moral law. For gambling to be considered a simple act of recreation, the virtue of prudence must be employed and scandal avoided.

On its face, it appears that Bennett may have failed to follow a part of his message that he professed to others. In *The Book of Virtues,* Bennett says, "We should know that too much of anything, even a good thing, may prove to be our undoing.... [We] need to set definite boundaries on our appetites." But does failing to do what is prudent, from time to time, lessen the truth of whatever message is being proclaimed?

Consider that no individual has done more to piously spread the word of Christianity than the apostle Paul. Yet, in Romans 7:19-20 we discover Paul's pretense: "The willing is ready at hand, but doing good is not. For I do not do the good I want, but I do the evil I do not want. Now if I do not do what I want, it is no longer I, but sin that dwells in me." Today, Paul is looked upon by many not as a moral hypocrite, but as an imperfect human being who dared to proclaim the truth.

Messages regarding moral clarity, in no event, should be delivered from moral high ground. After all, we are all fallible human beings—everyone makes mistakes. Therefore, it is easy for any messenger to fall from grace. It would be far worse if worthy messages like Bennett's were no longer heard. Syndicated columnist Cal Thomas said this of Bennett: "Like all of us, Bill Bennett suffers from certain vices. But that does not override the virtues he has proclaimed."

That night in Washington, Bennett joked that, as an Irish Catholic who was raised in Brooklyn, he would see a street fight and ask, "Is this a private fight or can anybody join in?"

I sincerely hope that Bennett, as well as many other flawed and caring Americans, will remain in the fight for those principles and ideals that make America and our global community better places to live. Liberty, spiritual capital, and a free market system cannot exist over the long-term without enduring values and ethical conduct. The biggest risk facing America and the Dream is not the intermittent failure to do what is right; it is the persistent indifference as to *what* is right. To awaken the American Dream, we need to understand and apply the foundational values of our nation, and work diligently to live them every day.

Reconnect With America's Founding Spirit

While many of the unalienable rights entrusted to us under the Declaration of Independence may be taken for granted today, that was not the case for the 56 men who signed that remarkable document. Overall, they were men of deep faith, and many were prosperous members of the colonial elite. These distinguished patriots courageously signed the Declaration, understanding that their property could be confiscated and, if captured, they could face execution.

Many paid a harsh price for their patriotism. Nearly one-third had their estates destroyed. Unfamiliar signers of significant wealth like Carter Braxton and Richard Morris supported the Revolutionary War with their own assets and died in relative poverty. Other men of financial means such as Richard Stockton and Arthur Middleton, who were taken prisoners by the British, likewise lost all that they had after their release. The price of the war forced John Hart to flee from the bedside of his dying wife. When he returned home after the war, he found his wife dead, his property destroyed, and his thirteen children gone.

These brave signers lived with a spirit that transcended all religious faiths, and, with integrity, they carried out the promises found in the last line of the Declaration of Independence: *"And for the support of this declaration, with a firm reliance on the protection of Divine Providence, we mutually pledge to each other our lives, our fortunes, and our sacred honor."*

America became a great nation precisely because its early settlers exhibited exceptional character. They lived out the American Dream seeking Divine Providence and pledging all that they had, believing that it was worth living and dying for to protect the virtues of freedom and liberty. They emptied themselves and, in many cases, laid down their lives and possessions for countless people they didn't know and for other generations to come.

Our Founding Fathers believed that the American Dream depended upon the strong character of its many diverse individuals. They understood that the Creator, who gave us our unalienable rights, requires virtue as the price for freedom and liberty. Liberty for them was not doing what they impulsively wanted to do. It was finding the courage to do what they needed to do after careful deliberation.

For our Founding Fathers, America was an emerging market economy, and capitalism was just a babe. If they could come back today, they would most likely be amazed by the financial capital that America has amassed in a little more than 200 years. On the other hand, it's hard to imagine that they wouldn't be troubled by the low level of spiritual capital found in today's American Dream.

From our country's inception to this very day, our republic has depended upon virtue, both private and public, for its survival. But as both George Washington and Thomas Paine pointed out long ago, "Virtue is not hereditary." Virtue must be taught, nurtured, and consciously passed on from one generation to the next.

In President Ronald Reagan's First Inaugural Address, he spoke of a man named Dr. Joseph Warren, and referred to him as "one of the greatest" among our Founding Fathers. Dr. Warren was a Harvard-educated medical doctor who became a Major General at the outset of the Revolutionary War. Instead of giving orders from a distance at Bunker Hill, he volunteered to fight alongside his men against the British onslaught. In doing so, Dr. Warren became the first high-ranking officer to fall in the war, when he was struck in the head by a musket ball that killed him instantly.

The night before Bunker Hill, Dr. Warren, as the President of the Massachusetts Congress, said to his countrymen, "Our country is in danger, but not to be despaired of.... On you depends the fortunes of America. You are to decide the important questions upon which rest the happiness and the liberty of millions yet unborn. Act worthy of yourselves."

The tragic events of 9/11 and the War Against Terrorism awakened the greatness of that founding spirit and our slumbering sense of patriotism. Our challenge, however, is to hold on to that selfless spirit, not only during wartime but long after it is over. Ultimately, we need to find a peaceful way to live together as one human family with our brothers and sisters around the globe. The principles of democracy, particularly in the Middle East, must be carefully molded around diverse cultures, with great respect for native traditions and religious beliefs.

Winning the War Against Terrorism will require more than just decisive military action. If we are to truly win the War, we must also fight to eradicate global poverty, educate humanity on the sanctity of life, and act in ways that support human dignity. The American Dream, grounded in love, is not America's message to the world; it is our Creator's message to humanity.

As we seek lives that are both rich and meaningful, we do so with the firm belief that we are God's greatest creation, and that we are here to make the world a better place. Love is the power necessary to do that, and our Creator is the source of all love. Our life's mission is to stay connected to that source and make its presence felt throughout the world. And despite all of its shortcomings, religious faith is a tremendous teacher and guardian of essential virtues that keep us allied to God. I could write a book about the negative things concerning religious faith, but I could more easily fill a library with all the good it has done for people.

If we are to achieve and pass on the American Dream from one generation to the next, it will be because of our commitment to virtues and the production of spiritual capital in a free market system. We don't really own material possessions anyway. We merely have use of them for a while.

We only have possession of what is inside our souls, where the values that became our life's virtues were first conceived. And when we are successful in this regard, we will be leaving something dear for those who live on and for the millions yet unborn. We will have acted in a manner worthy of ourselves and awakened the American Dream—making it come alive for generations to come.

"We may ignore but we can nowhere evade, the presence of God. The world is crowded with Him. He walks everywhere incognito. And the incognito is not always easy to penetrate. The real labor is to remember to attend. In fact to come awake. Still more to remain awake."

—C. S. Lewis

Share
AWAKEN THE AMERICAN DREAM
With Others

To purchase or order single copies
of the book, visit your local bookstore or
anywhere books are sold.

For more information about how
Charlie Douglas can help your company,
school, or organization, visit him on the web
or contact him by email:

Douglas@awakenthedream.com
www.awakenthedream.com
See website for suggested reading
and references.

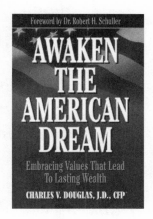

Set the Stage for a Great Meeting With Charlie Douglas, Professional Advisor and Author

Charlie Is Available for:
Keynote Addresses • Private Client Seminars
Values-Based Planning

Charlie Offers Professional Advice for:
Comprehensive Financial Planning
Crafting Mission Statements • Goal-Setting

Quantity Sales of
AWAKEN THE AMERICAN DREAM

Awaken The American Dream and all other *Possibility Press* books are available at special quantity discounts when purchased in bulk by individuals, corporations, organizations, schools, and special interest groups. They may be used for education, motivation, sales promotions, premiums, fundraisers, reselling, and gifts. Call *Possibility Press* at (717) 566-0468 (9-5 ET/M-F), or email us at possibilitypress@aol.com.

In the Final Analysis

"*People are often unreasonable, illogical and self-centered; forgive them anyway. If you are kind, people may accuse you of selfish, ulterior motives; be kind anyway. If you are successful, you will win some false friends and some true enemies; succeed anyway. If you are honest and frank, people may cheat you; be honest and frank anyway. What you spend years building, someone may destroy overnight; build anyway. If you find serenity and happiness, they may be jealous; be happy anyway. The good you do today, people will often forget tomorrow; do good anyway. Give the world the best you have, and it may never be enough; give the world the best you have anyway. You see, in the final analysis, it is all between you and God; it was never between you and them anyway.*"

Based on the *Paradoxical Commandments*
—Dr. Kent M. Keith

Who Is Charlie Douglas?

Charlie Douglas is a professional advisor, author, and life-long student of America's principled heritage. He is passionate about awakening the American Dream. His skilled delivery and powerful message make him a frequent lecturer and keynote speaker for professional organizations, church groups, and other associations.

As an attorney and CERTIFIED FINANCIAL PLANNER™, Charlie has been counseling high-net-worth individuals for almost 20 years, regarding wealth-related issues. Today, he helps others pursue a revitalized American Dream and pass on a rich legacy through values-based and multi-generational planning.

His diverse experience base and willingness to think beyond traditional planning concepts put him at the cutting edge of comprehensive planning. As a skilled facilitator, Charlie also helps clients uncover their personal histories, determine core values, and craft indispensable mission statements that support the pursuit of truly lasting wealth.

Writing *Awaken The American Dream* has given Charlie a unique perspective and a greater passion for America and its future. He believes the ongoing War Against Terrorism provides us with a window of opportunity to take stock and begin anew. All we need is the courage and conviction to take action in accordance with the wisdom forged from trying times.

In addition to writing *Awaken The American Dream*, Charlie is also a contributing author to *Walking With The Wise*, which features such notables as: Brian Tracy, Zig Ziglar, Mark Victor Hansen, Cynthia Kersey, Deepak Chopra, and many other best-selling authors and influential Americans.

Charlie lives in Atlanta, GA with his wife, Lori, where they are active in their church. He is also a devoted supporter of Mother Teresa's Missionaries of Charity, The Carter Center, Empower America, and The Heritage Foundation. Visit Charlie on the web at www.awakenthedream.com.

Acknowledgment

To the many people who have helped me along the way with their willingness to listen to my ideas, lend their support, and read "one more" draft. The list of those who assisted me in this journey is far too long to mention, but a few special people come to mind: Leo Grant, Ally Beasley, Steve Levy, Joe Kilbarger, Dennis and Jayne Horn, Dee and Greg Cabana, Harold Metzel, Sue Cassidy, Shaun Cassidy, Deacon Harold Gourgues, and Gavin de Becker. So many others gave their heartfelt input too (including my father!)—please know that I am sincerely grateful.

To the Sisters at Missionaries of Charity, thank you for continuing to show me the direction toward love through the servant of God, Mother Teresa of Calcutta.

To my loving parents, Marilyn and Charles, and their many years of being there for me, please know how much I love you both.

To my lovely wife, Lori, who is entrusted with the responsibility of helping me get to heaven—I know it's a lot of work. I love you, honey, and look forward to holding your hand and praying together each night. Thank you for the gift of believing in me.

To the staff at Possibility Press (Mike, Marjie, and Janet), a special thank you for rolling up your sleeves and making this dream come alive. Your mission of helping others to make a difference in the world is a noble one. The world needs more publishers like you.

And to God, the greatest thanks of all, whose loving presence and inspiration helped me not to give up. My labors were those of a wanting messenger, but You are the message of the American Dream.